The Law Commission
Consultation Paper No 188

and

The Scottish Law Commission
Discussion Paper No 139

CONSUMER REMEDIES FOR FAULTY GOODS

A Joint Consultation Paper

ISBN: 9780118404570

THE LAW COMMISSION
AND
THE SCOTTISH LAW COMMISSION

The Law Commission and the Scottish Law Commission were set up by section 1 of the Law Commissions Act 1965 for the purpose of promoting the reform of the law.

The Law Commissioners are:

> The Right Honourable Lord Justice Etherton, *Chairman*
> Professor Elizabeth Cooke
> Mr David Hertzell
> Professor Jeremy Horder
> Kenneth Parker QC

The Chief Executive of the Law Commission is William Arnold and its offices are at Steel House, 11 Tothill Street, London SW1H 9LJ.

The Scottish Law Commissioners are:

> The Honourable Lord Drummond Young, *Chairman*
> Professor George L Gretton
> Patrick Layden QC, TD
> Professor Joseph M Thomson
> Colin J Tyre QC

The Chief Executive of the Scottish Law Commission is Malcolm McMillan and its offices are at 140 Causewayside, Edinburgh EH9 1PR.

This joint consultation paper, completed on 20 October 2008, is circulated for comment and criticism only. It does not represent the final views of the two Law Commissions.

We would be grateful for comments on the proposals before **2 February 2009**. Please send comments to the Law Commission either –

By email to:

commercialandcommon@lawcommission.gsi.gov.uk; or

By post to:

Donna Birthwright, Law Commission, Steel House, 11 Tothill Street, London SW1H 9LJ

Tel: 020-3334-0284 / Fax: 020-3334-0201

It would be helpful if, where possible, comments sent by post could also be sent on disk, or by email to the above address, in any commonly used format.

As the Law Commission will be the recipient of responses, we will treat all responses as public documents in accordance with the Freedom of Information Act and we may attribute comments and include a list of all respondents' names in any final report we publish. Those who wish to submit a confidential response should contact the Commission before sending the response. We will disregard automatic confidentiality disclaimers generated by an IT system.

This consultation paper is available free of charge at:

http://www.lawcom.gov.uk/consumer_remedies.htm and
http://www.scotlawcom.gov.uk/downloads/dps/dp139.pdf

THE LAW COMMISSION

THE SCOTTISH LAW COMMISSION

CONSUMER REMEDIES FOR FAULTY GOODS

CONTENTS

Appendix C (European Consumer Centre questionnaire) and Appendix D (Comparative consumer law) are available online at www.lawcom.gov.uk and www.scotlawcom.gov.uk.

TABLE OF ABBREVIATIONS

BERR   Department for Business, Enterprise and Regulatory Reform

CSD   Directive 1999/44/EC of 25 May 1999 on Certain Aspects of the Sale of Consumer Goods and Associated Guarantees, 1999 OJ L 171 12-16

DTI   Department of Trade and Industry

FDS   FDS International Limited

OFT   Office of Fair Trading

SoGA   Sale of Goods Act 1979

UCPD   Directive 2005/29/EC (Unfair Commercial Practices Directive)

PART 1
INTRODUCTION

1.1 In December 2007, the Department for Business, Enterprise and Regulatory Reform (BERR) asked the Law Commission and Scottish Law Commission to review the legal remedies available to consumers when they buy faulty goods. This followed criticism by the Davidson Review in 2006 that the existing law is over complicated.

1.2 It is fairly clear what standards goods should meet. There is general awareness that goods must, for example, be of satisfactory quality, and correspond with their description.[1] However, there is less understanding about the remedies available to consumers if goods do not meet these terms. There are effectively two legal regimes: the traditional UK remedies have been overlain by the scheme set out in the EU Consumer Sales Directive (CSD). This makes the law difficult for consumers and retailers to understand, and can generate unnecessary disputes.

1.3 Although this review was sparked by UK concerns, it is being conducted against the backdrop of the European Commission's review of the consumer directives. On 8 October 2008, the European Commission published a proposal for a new directive on consumer rights. Among other things, this recommends major changes to the law on consumer remedies for faulty goods. BERR is currently seeking views on the European Commission's proposal.[2]

1.4 Our Consultation Paper is not a direct response to what the European Commission has proposed. Instead, we look in more depth at the principles behind an appropriate scheme of consumer remedies, considering the circumstances when consumers should be entitled to a full refund, rather than a repair or a replacement. However, we hope that this paper and the responses to it will inform the debate on this subject, at both a European and national level.

1.5 We seek views on our questions and proposals for reform by **2 February 2009**. Please send responses to the Law Commission at the address given at the front of this paper.

1.6 We urge stakeholders to consider both our paper and the BERR consultation on the European Commission's proposal. However, stakeholders only need draft one joint reply. We have agreed that any responses sent to us will be copied to BERR, and responses sent to BERR will be copied to us to inform our consultation (unless respondents ask that they should not be, in either case). The deadline for both consultations is the same.

TERMS OF REFERENCE

1.7 Our terms of reference are:

---

[1] For a description of the implied terms of quality and correspondence, see below, para 2.7.

[2] BERR's consultation paper on the proposed directive is available at www.berr.gov.uk.

(1) To examine the existing consumer remedies under the Sale of Goods Act 1979, the Supply of Goods (Implied Terms) Act 1973 and the Supply of Goods and Services Act 1982 for goods which do not conform to contract, together with related issues; and to consider the case for simplification and rationalisation, so far as possible, to make the law easier for all users to understand and use, and to reduce burdens on business;

(2) Following full consultation with relevant stakeholders, to make appropriate recommendations within the current framework of EU law; and

(3) To advise BERR on issues raised in the course of the EU review of the consumer acquis relating to the reform of the CSD and/or remedies for breach of a consumer contract.

1.8 Given that problems with faulty goods occur regularly in everyday life, it is particularly important that the law in this area is simple and easy to use. Our aim is to simplify the remedies available to consumers, bring the law into line with accepted good practice, and provide appropriate remedies which allow consumers to participate with confidence in the market place.

CRITICISMS OF THE LAW

1.9 The domestic law relating to the sale of goods is set out in the Sale of Goods Act 1979 (SoGA). Essentially, it allows the consumer to reject faulty goods and claim a full refund. However, the right is lost once the consumer is deemed to have accepted them, which may happen "after the lapse of a reasonable time".[3] Thereafter, the consumer has the right to damages only. In 2002, the UK implemented the CSD, which sets out a separate regime of remedies. Initially, consumers may ask for a repair or replacement. If this is impossible or disproportionate, or if a repair or replacement cannot be provided without unreasonable delay or significant inconvenience, the consumer may move to second tier remedies. These are rescission or reduction in price.[4]

1.10 The domestic law has been criticised for its uncertainty: in particular, for its conflicting case law over what constitutes "a reasonable time" to reject goods.[5] In addition, the EU remedies have their own uncertainties, for example, over what amounts to "significant inconvenience". These problems are compounded by the fact that the two separate regimes co-exist, using different language and concepts and imposing different burdens of proof. As a result, SoGA has been described as "a disjointed, often incoherent, amalgam".[6]

---

[3] SoGA, s 35(4).

[4] The Sale and Supply of Goods to Consumer Regulations 2002 (SI 2002 No 3045) amend the SoGA and Supply of Goods and Services Act 1982. They implement Directive 1999/44/EC on certain aspects of the sale of consumer goods and associated guarantees, Official Journal L171 of 07.07.1999 p 12.

[5] See *Bernstein v Pamson Motors* [1987] 2 All ER 220 and *Clegg v Olle Andersson* (2003) 1 All ER (Comm) 721.

[6] L Miller, "The Common Frame of Reference and the feasibility of a common contract law in Europe" [2007] *Journal of Business Law* 378.

1.11   There are now (at least[7]) six remedies for consumers if they buy faulty goods. Domestic law provides for the right to reject and damages, while the CSD provides for repair, replacement, rescission or reduction in price. In some cases the distinction between these remedies is subtle. Both the right to reject and rescission involve returning goods and refunding the purchase price, though rescission may also require the buyer to give an allowance for the use they have had from the product.[8] However, the domestic and EU regimes stem from different conceptual approaches. As Miller points out,[9] the common law assumes that when a contract goes wrong, it should be ended as soon as possible (hence a quick right to reject). The CSD, however, draws on a civil law approach, which strives to get the parties to abide by their obligations.

The Davidson Review

1.12   This project was recommended by the Davidson Review, set up by the then Chancellor of the Exchequer, Gordon Brown, in 2005, under the aegis of the Better Regulation Executive. The Review looked at the way EU Directives were implemented – considering problems of "gold-plating" (where domestic legislation goes further than Directives require) and "double-banking" (where EU regulations are superimposed on domestic legislation, causing unacceptable levels of complexity and confusion). The remedies available to consumers for faulty goods were cited as an example of double-banking.

1.13   In November 2006, the Davidson Review recommended that the Department of Trade and Industry should ask the two Law Commissions to produce a joint report "on the reform and simplification of remedies available to consumers relating to the sale and supply of goods".

1.14   The Davidson Review found that following the implementation of the CSD, the remedies available to consumers for faulty goods were too complicated, making it unclear how the choice should be made between the various remedies available. This followed representations by some retailers about difficulties in training sales staff to know when consumers could return faulty goods. It was argued that this led to a lack of shared understanding between consumers and retailers, and increased amounts of litigation. Disputes usually arose in relation to expensive and technical products where faults might not surface until later on and there was more money at stake for both parties.[10]

---

[7]   G Howells and S Weatherill, *Consumer Protection Law* (2nd ed 2005) p 201, suggests that the availability of specific performance in SoGA, s 52 is in addition to the Directive rights. There is also the possibility of another kind of rejection-based liability under a collateral contract for a repair: *J & H Ritchie Ltd v Lloyd Ltd* 2007 SC (HL) 89; [2007] 1 WLR 670; [2007] 2 All ER 353.

[8]   When a consumer rescinds a contract, they must make an allowance for the use they have had of the goods, but it is not clear how this is to be valued.

[9]   L Miller, "The Common Frame of Reference and the feasibility of a common contract law in Europe" [2007] *Journal of Business Law* 378.

[10]   Davidson Review, *Final Report* (November 2006) para 3.20.

THE CONTEXT OF REFORM

1.15 There is now considerable interest in reforming and simplifying consumer law within both the EU and the UK. This project is one of several reviews, which we outline below.

The European Commission's review of the consumer acquis

1.16 In 2004 the European Commission launched a review of the eight consumer protection directives which already exist within the EU. These are referred to collectively as "the consumer acquis".[11] The Commission published a green paper in February 2007,[12] and a summary of responses later that year.[13]

1.17 Then, on 8 October 2008, the European Commission published a proposal for a new directive on consumer rights.[14] This is intended to reform four existing EU consumer directives including the CSD, and it proposes significant changes to the areas covered by this paper.

1.18 The proposed directive is a maximum harmonisation measure, which would mean that member states would not be able to provide greater or lesser rights in any field falling within the scope of the directive. In the area of consumer remedies for faulty goods, this would result in reductions to consumer rights in the UK. For example, the initial right to reject would be lost, and rescission would not be allowed for defects deemed to be minor. We summarise these proposals at the end of Part 2,[15] and refer to them in Part 8.

1.19 BERR has published a consultation paper on the proposed directive. The consultation is open until 2 February 2009 and is available at www.berr.gov.uk.[16] As part of our terms of reference, BERR has asked us to advise them on the issues raised in the course of the EU review which relate to the reform of the CSD. This means that responses to both the BERR consultation and this Consultation Paper will inform the UK's negotiating strategy on reform of consumer remedies at EU level and policy-making at a domestic level.

---

[11] The term borrows from the French word, *acquis*, meaning "that which has been acquired".

[12] http://ec.europa.eu/consumers/cons_int/safe_shop/acquis/green-paper_cons_acquis_en.pdf.

[13] http://ec.europa.eu/consumers/cons_int/safe_shop/acquis/acquis_working_doc.pdf.

[14] COM (2008) 614/3: see http://ec.europa.eu/consumers/rights/cons_acquis_en.htm.

[15] See para 2.66 onwards.

[16] Further information on the proposed directive and BERR's EU consumer policy is available on the BERR website at:
http://www.berr.gov.uk/whatwedo/consumers/policy/eu/index.html.

The Draft Common Frame of Reference and Principles of European Law on Sales

1.20 There are other interesting developments in the field of European consumer law. The Draft Common Frame of Reference (DCFR) was published in January 2008.[17] This document has been produced by academics, and is currently being considered by the European Commission. It helps define the important concepts that lie behind the proposed directive, including, for example, the definition of a "sale". It is intended that the DCFR will assist the European Commission in developing a Common Frame of Reference for European Contract Law. This will be a tool kit of definitions, general principles and model rules for contract law including consumer contract law.

1.21 The Principles of European Law on Sales is another academic work, designed to complement the Principles of European Contract Law. It draws on common elements from the law of sales in all the member states to create a single code that mirrors the national regimes. Again, we have used this to inform our views.

BERR's review of consumer protection legislation

1.22 At a domestic level, the Government, through BERR, has launched a review of the UK's consumer protection regime.[18] This examines how existing legislation and its enforcement can be simplified and made more flexible and investigates how consumers can be better informed of their rights.

1.23 In May 2008 BERR issued a Call for Evidence.[19] We intend to feed our own recommendations into that review, which will be influenced both by this consultation and by BERR's consultation on the proposed directive.

THE SCOPE OF THIS CONSULTATION PAPER

1.24 This Consultation Paper is not intended to be a comprehensive review of the law of the sale and supply of goods. It focuses only on the remedies available to the consumer, and only for goods which "do not conform to contract".

---

[17] The Interim Outline Edition of the Principles, Definitions and Model Rules of European Private Law Draft Common Frame of Reference by the Study Group on a European Civil Code and the Research Group on EC Private Law (Acquis Group).

[18] See http://www.berr.gov.uk/whatwedo/bre/reviewing-regulation/protecting-consumers/page44093.html.

[19] BERR, *Consumer Law Review Call for Evidence* (May 2008).

Non-conforming goods

1.25 Goods do not conform to contract where the retailer sells or supplies goods in breach of an express or implied contractual term.[20] In particular, goods do not conform if they do not correspond with the description by which they are sold, if they are not of satisfactory quality or fit for their purpose, or if they do not correspond with the sample by which they are sold.[21] Furthermore, goods may be delivered late, contrary to an express term of the contract, or the wrong quantity of goods may be delivered (either too few or too many), so that the delivery does not correspond with what has been agreed.

1.26 In this Consultation Paper, we refer to non-conforming goods as "faulty goods". Most of the examples we give are about household goods, cars or toys that break, and are therefore not of satisfactory quality. These seem to be the most common problems in practice, and they provide an illustration to which readers can relate.

1.27 However, non-conformity goes wider than this. Sour milk or corked wine would not conform to contract, nor would a book with pages missing. Goods may not be fit for their purpose, such as where a consumer asks for a drill bit suitable for masonry, and is sold one suitable only for wood. The concept also applies where goods do not correspond with their description, or where they are different from the samples shown in the shop. For example, seeds may be a different variety from the one described, or the retailer may deliver tiles that are a different colour from the one the consumer chose in the shop. We also consider examples where the retailer delivers too much (a magnum of champagne rather than a standard bottle) or too little (12 bottles rather than 48). Finally, the delivery might be of the right amount and the right quality, but arrive late (as where the champagne arrives the day after the wedding).

Issues not considered

1.28 It may be useful to clarify what we are not looking at in this paper. We are not considering services, only goods. We are not looking at the standards goods should meet, only at the remedies available when the standards are not met.

1.29 Nor do we consider the special rights given to consumers to cancel contracts when they buy through distance selling methods (such as over the telephone or on the internet) or in their own homes. These rights apply equally to non-faulty goods, so are conceptually distinct from remedies for breach of contract. However, they do form part of the factual backdrop against which the remedies for faulty goods need to be judged. In Part 2 we summarise these cancellation rights briefly. We explain that the abolition of the right to reject goods would have a greater effect on shop sales than on (say) online sales, where the European Commission has proposed that the consumer should have the right to cancel within 14 days, whether or not goods are faulty.

---

[20] SoGA, s 48F states that "goods do not conform to a contract of sale if there is, in relation to the goods, a breach of an express term of the contract or a term implied by section 13, 14 or 15" (see below).

[21] SoGA, ss 13, 14 and 15. For more details, and the equivalent terms in other supply contracts, see para 2.7 and footnotes.

1.30 Finally, as we explain below, we have decided not to look at the special problems raised in software contracts, or the remedies that should be available where the retailer sells a product for which they do not have good title.

Software

1.31 The CSD does not cover computer software.[22] Under UK law, the classification of software is not entirely clear.[23] It seems that software on disks may constitute "goods" for the purposes of SoGA, but that downloaded software does not.[24] Our initial discussions with stakeholders highlighted that there are several questions which are peculiar to software, such as the nature of the implied term of quality, liability for consequential loss and how far this may be excluded by an end-user licence agreement. We think they are too far-reaching to deal with in this paper.

1.32 We understand that BERR is considering this issue in the course of their review of consumer protection.[25] Depending on BERR's conclusions, we may return to this subject.

Remedies for breach of the implied terms of title

1.33 Occasionally consumers find that the goods they have bought turn out to be stolen, or subject to an undisclosed lease or hire purchase agreement. Under SoGA, this is a breach of an implied term of the contract.[26] The remedies for breach of this implied term can be complex, and raise difficult issues.[27]

---

[22] CSD, Art 1(2) defines consumer goods as "tangible movable items". (The French language version of the Directive defines consumer goods as "tout objet mobilier corporel" which better fits the Scots law view, where tangible means corporeal.) The European Commission raised the issue of whether this should be changed, but they are not proceeding with proposals at present: see *Green Paper on the Consumer Acquis* COM (2006) 744 final, para 3.1.

[23] S Green and D Saidov, "Software as Goods" [2007] *Journal of Business Law* 161.

[24] According to Sir Iain Glidewell in *St Albans City v International Computer Limited* [1996] 4 All ER 481, though *Beta Computers (Europe) Ltd v Adobe Systems (Europe) Ltd* 1996 SLT 604; [1996] SCLR 587 suggests that even if software is provided on a disk it should not be classified as a good.

[25] See BERR, *Consumer Law Review Call for Evidence* (May 2008) Question 7, p 18.

[26] SoGA, s 12 sets out implied terms that the seller has the right to sell the goods, and that the goods are free from any undisclosed charge or encumbrance. Similar terms are implied into contracts for the supply of goods (Supply of Goods and Services Act 1982, ss 2, 7, 11B and 11H) and hire purchase (Supply of Goods (Implied Terms) Act 1973, s 8).

[27] Suppose, for example, a consumer unwittingly bought a stolen car from a dealer, and used if for a year before the owner repossesses it. One difficult issue is whether the consumer should be entitled to a full refund (on the grounds that the seller as totally failed to provide what was contracted for) or whether the consumer should give some allowance for the use they have had from the car. It is not clear how far the European Commission's proposals for maximum harmonisation are intended to affect this area.

1.34 In initial consultations, traders suggested that we should look at the remedies alongside the substantive rules about when an innocent buyer should receive good title to goods which are subject to a third party claim. In 2005, the Law Commission proposed such a project as part of its ninth programme of law reform, though it was deferred. In its tenth programme, in 2008, the Law Commission said it would consider the project as part of its eleventh programme, to start in 2011.[28]

1.35 We have therefore decided not to look at remedies for defects in title in the course of this project. We hope at some stage in the future to tackle the long-standing problem of how to protect innocent buyers who buy goods which turn out to be subject to the claims of finance companies and other third parties.

SCOPE FOR REFORM

1.36 Clearly, any domestic legislation will need to comply with the relevant European directive. If the directive remains a minimum harmonisation measure, the UK would not be permitted unilaterally to remove the rights specified in that directive. If the directive becomes a maximum harmonisation measure, the UK would not be permitted to deviate from it, either by adding or removing rights.

1.37 This means that our proposals should be seen primarily as part of the debate or negotiation within the EU about how the CSD should be reformed. However, if the replacement to the CSD remains a minimum harmonisation measure, the UK could add remedies, and we consider what those additions should be.

WORK SO FAR

1.38 In February 2008, we issued a joint introductory paper which explained the scope of this project and summarised the issues. Between February and April 2008, we talked to a range of stakeholders with experience in this field, including companies and organisations representing retailers, manufacturers and consumers.[29] We are very grateful to them for their assistance. The feedback from those meetings has helped us to formulate our views and proposals.

1.39 We commissioned qualitative market research into consumer attitudes and understanding of this area of law. This research was carried out by FDS International. Their report was completed in April 2008 and is attached at Appendix A.

1.40 We have also undertaken comparative research. We asked a range of experts to advise us on the law in other jurisdictions and worked with European Consumer Centres to see how the law works in practice.[30]

---

[28] Tenth Programme of Law Reform, Law Com 311, 2008, p 31.

[29] See Appendix B for a list of people and organisations we met, or who otherwise submitted information.

[30] This is set out in Part 6 and Appendix D (available on our website at www.lawcom.gov.uk and www.scotlawcom.gov.uk).

THE IMPORTANCE OF CONSUMER PROTECTION LEGISLATION

1.41 Surveys show that consumer problems are extremely common. It is estimated that consumers annually encounter around 10 million problems with goods they have bought.[31] The great majority of consumers who complain do so to the retailer or service provider, without outside help.[32] Only a few take it further, and very few end up in court.[33]

1.42 Given that so many consumers contact retailers directly, it is particularly important that the law should be accessible. Consumers need a broad understanding of the remedies to which they may be entitled, while sales managers and consumer advisers need more detailed knowledge. The law should be simple enough for retail staff and advisers to be trained in what they need to know, without imposing unnecessary burdens on businesses. In the absence of full understanding, both sides are likely to reach a partial and inaccurate view of what the law requires, aggravating the potential for disputes and litigation.

1.43 However, the need for clarity should be balanced against the need to retain sufficient flexibility to deal with a wide range of consumer problems fairly, in a way that meets the legitimate expectations of both parties. Where there is a mismatch between lay views of what consumers are entitled to and what the law provides, consumer confidence may suffer.

1.44 In 1999 a Government white paper explained that knowledgeable, demanding consumers are also good for the economy.[34] They drive up standards and encourage innovation and competition. The more confident consumers are, the more likely they are to make purchases and encourage economic growth. In Part 9 we set out the economic benefits of good consumer law.

The market place

1.45 As this project progressed, we were made aware of how much consumers rely on shops' policies for information about their rights. Consumers' expectations are heavily influenced by retailers' returns policies, in particular the voluntary "no-quibble money-back" policies offered by high street retailers, which usually allow returns for whatever reason within a month or thereabouts. Returns policies are also a major factor influencing consumers' decisions about where to shop.[35]

1.46 It would seem that consumers' expectations of their rights have been raised by these returns policies. In a reciprocal fashion, consumers' expectations also drive retailers' returns policies, as retailers compete for custom, and are aware that such policies affect purchasing decisions. A large proportion of returns are dealt with under voluntary policies rather than the strict letter of the law.

[31] OFT, *Consumer Detriment* (2000). Not all these problems will necessarily involve a legal cause for action.

[32] See OFT, *Consumer Detriment* (2008) and P Pleasance and others, *Causes of Action* (2006). We summarise the evidence on this in Part 5.

[33] H Genn, *Paths to Justice* (1999) found that only 1% of consumer problems were dealt with in a court hearing.

[34] DTI, *Modern Markets: Confident Consumers*, July 1999.

[35] FDS Report, Appendix A.

1.47 Nevertheless, the law provides an essential minimum standard. Not all shops have voluntary returns policies; in some circumstances the returns policy is less generous than the law; and there are particular difficulties where a consumer attempts to return faulty goods in circumstances which fall outside the terms of the shop's returns policy.

THE STRUCTURE OF THIS PAPER

1.48 This Consultation Paper is divided into a further nine parts:

(1) Part 2 provides a brief account of the current law, together with a summary of the European Commission's main proposals for reform;

(2) Part 3 looks in more detail at the "right to reject" in UK law, and how it has been interpreted in the case law;

(3) Part 4 summarises the research we commissioned from FDS in the course of this review, looking at consumers' perceptions of the current remedies;

(4) Part 5 summarises other recent empirical research into consumer problems;

(5) Part 6 provides a brief account of consumer remedies in the following jurisdictions: France; Germany; Ireland; the USA; and New Zealand. It concludes with the results of our questionnaire to European Consumer Centres, outlining how consumer remedies work in practice in 17 EU member states;

(6) Part 7 explores the complexities of the current UK legal regime, showing why we think that some reform is needed;

(7) Part 8 sets out our proposals for reform;

(8) Part 9 assesses the impact of our proposals;

(9) Part 10 lists our provisional proposals and questions.

1.49 Appendix A contains a copy of the consumer research from FDS. Appendix B provides a list of the people and organisations who met us or who sent submissions from January to April 2008.

1.50 Further appendices are to be found on our website (www.lawcom.gov.uk and www.scotlawcom.gov.uk). Appendix C is the questionnaire sent to European Consumer Centres; and Appendix D provides a more detailed account of consumer remedies in France, Germany, Ireland, USA and New Zealand.

ACKNOWLEDGEMENTS

1.51 We have received very valuable help from a group of advisors to the project: Dr Christian Twigg-Flesner of the University of Hull; Professor Geraint Howells of the University of Lancaster; W Cowan H Ervine of the University of Dundee; Professor Simon Whittaker of St John's College, Oxford; Professor Cynthia Hawes of the University of Canterbury, New Zealand; Professor Hans-W Micklitz and Kai P Purnhagen of the European University Institute in Florence; Professor John Adams of the University of Sheffield; and the UK European Consumer Centre.

1.52 We are also grateful to the many business and consumer representatives who have contributed to the project. We would like to acknowledge the particularly helpful contributions of: the British Retail Consortium; the Confederation of British Industry; Intellect – Consumer Electronics Council; the Retail Motor Industry Federation; the Scottish Motor Trade Association; Which?; the Local Authorities Co-ordinators of Regulatory Services; Citizens Advice; Consumer Direct; and the Scottish Consumer Council.

PART 2
CURRENT REMEDIES FOR FAULTY GOODS

INTRODUCTION

2.1 Historically, in England and Wales, the buyer of faulty goods had two options. If done quickly enough, the buyer could reject the goods, terminate the contract, and demand a refund. Alternatively, or if too much time had passed, the buyer could seek compensation for the seller's breach of contract. These two remedies emerged from English case law and were included in the Sale of Goods Act 1893. The 1893 Act also amended Scots law to provide similar remedies in Scotland.[1] These remedies are still applicable today, with a few changes, through the Sale of Goods Act 1979 (SoGA).

2.2 For consumers, the historical "right to reject" and damages are now joined by remedies that have their origin in EU legislation. Since 2003 the consumer buyer of faulty goods has been able to demand that the seller repair or replace the goods or, failing that, to rescind the contract or receive a reduction in the purchase price.[2]

2.3 This Part is intended as an overview of the current regime. Part 3 focuses on the right to reject, in particular the reasonable period for examining goods.

Sales and other contracts to supply goods

2.4 The law makes a distinction between sales of goods, and other contracts to supply goods. Section 2 of SoGA sets out the definition of a "sale":

> A contract of sale is a contract by which the seller transfers or agrees to transfer the property in goods to the buyer for a money consideration, called the price.[3]

2.5 This definition does not include;

(1) contracts for hire or hire purchase (which do not necessarily transfer property in goods); or

(2) contracts for barter or exchange (which do not involve money); or

(3) contracts for work and materials (such as a fitted kitchen), where the contract is mainly for work or services, and the supply of materials is incidental to its main purpose.[4]

---

[1] For further details of the changes brought about to Scots law in 1893, see para 3.5.

[2] Directive 1999/44/EC on certain aspects of the sale of consumer goods and associated guarantees, Official Journal L171 of 07.07.1999 p 12, implemented by the Sale and Supply of Goods to Consumer Regulations 2002. These Regulations came into force on 31 March 2003.

[3] SoGA, s 2(1).

[4] See *Benjamin's Sale of Goods* (7th ed 2006) para 1-041.

2.6 There are important differences between the remedies available when goods are sold and when they are supplied under other contracts. We start by discussing sales. The remedies available for other supply contracts are set out in paragraphs 2.47 to 2.59.

"FAULTY GOODS"

2.7 In this Consultation Paper we do not intend to revisit the question of when goods should be considered "faulty", because they do not conform to contract. This was an issue that was considered in our 1987 Report,[5] which led to amendments to SoGA. This Consultation Paper is concerned with the remedies available to a consumer where:

(1) goods are sold by description, and they do not correspond with the description;[6]

(2) goods are sold by sample, and they do not correspond with the sample;[7]

(3) goods are not of satisfactory quality;[8]

(4) goods are not fit for the buyer's purpose, where the buyer has made that purpose known to the seller;[9]

(5) the wrong quantity is provided;[10]

(6) goods are delivered late; or

(7) goods do not conform to another express term of the contract.[11]

2.8 In practice, consumers are mainly concerned about the problems caused when goods are not of satisfactory quality, not as described or not fit for their purpose. Typical examples are where electrical goods do not work, or shoes fall apart. However, we also consider, briefly, what remedies are available when the trader delivers the wrong quantity, or when goods are delivered late.

---

[5] Sale and Supply of Goods (1987) Law Com No 160; Scot Law Com No 104.

[6] For sales contracts, see SoGA, s 13. For other supply contracts, see Supply of Goods and Services Act 1982, ss 3, 8, 11C and 11I; and for hire purchase contracts, see Supply of Goods (Implied Terms) Act 1973, s 9A.

[7] SoGA, s 15. See also Supply of Goods and Services Act 1982, ss 5, 10,11E and 11K; and Supply of Goods (Implied Terms) Act 1973, s 11.

[8] SoGA, s 14. Factors relevant to the quality of the goods include fitness for the purposes normally required of such goods and fitness for any particular purposes for which the goods were bought, and of which the seller knew. See also Supply of Goods and Services Act 1982, ss 4, 9, 11D and 11J; and Supply of Goods (Implied Terms) Act 1973, s 10.

[9] SoGA, s 14(3).

[10] Above, s 30.

[11] Above, s 48F.

SALES CONTRACTS: THE TRADITIONAL UK REMEDIES

The "right to reject"

2.9   SoGA gives the buyer a right to examine the goods following delivery.[12] A consumer who examines the goods and discovers that they are faulty is entitled to reject the goods and to bring the contract to an end. This entitles the consumer to refuse to pay for the goods, or to a refund of any money paid to the seller.

2.10 The rejection of the goods and the termination of the contract are separate concepts.[13] There are circumstances where the rejection of goods will not be followed by the termination of the contract.[14] In this Consultation Paper, however, we use the term "the right to reject" as a shorthand term to include both the rejection of faulty goods and the refund to the consumer of any money paid. This is done for simplicity of exposition.

2.11 In England and Wales, in non-consumer sales, the buyer must show that the defects in the goods are "not so slight that rejection would be unreasonable".[15] In consumer sales, however, there is no such requirement. Any defect which constitutes a breach of the "satisfactory quality" requirement allows the consumer to reject the goods, unless they have been "accepted".

2.12 The same effect is achieved in Scots law. For there to be a right to reject in any contract of sale in Scots law, the breach must be material.[16] In consumer sales contracts, however, a breach by the seller of any express or implied term that goods are of satisfactory quality (or correspond to their description or sample) is deemed to be material.[17] The provisions on "acceptance" apply equally to Scotland.

2.13 As we explain in more detail in Part 3, goods can be accepted in three ways:[18]

(1)   Where the buyer intimates to the seller that the goods have been accepted;

(2)   Where the buyer does something with the goods that is inconsistent with the seller's ownership of the goods; or

(3)   Where, after a lapse of a reasonable time, the buyer retains the goods without telling the seller that the goods have been rejected.

---

[12] This is done in two ways. SoGA, s 34 requires the seller "on request to afford the buyer a reasonable opportunity of examining the goods". Even without a request, however, the buyer effectively is given a reasonable time to examine the goods because he will not be deemed to have accepted the goods until that time has passed: SoGA, s 35.

[13] See s 11(3) of SoGA, and s 48D(2)(a) and s 48D(2)(b) which refer respectively to rejection and termination of the contract in England, Wales and Northern Ireland and rejection and treating the contract as repudiated in Scotland.

[14] See R Bradgate and F White, "Rejection and Termination in Contracts for the Sale of Goods" in J Birds, R Bradgate and C Villers (eds), *Termination of Contracts* (1995).

[15] SoGA, s 15A(1).

[16] Above, s 15B(1)(b).

[17] Above, s 15B(2).

[18] Above, s 35.

2.14 The most common form of acceptance is method 3, where the consumer is deemed to have accepted the goods because the reasonable time for rejecting them has elapsed. A consumer wishing to exercise the right to reject goods must do so quickly. The exact length of the reasonable time depends on the facts of the case, and there is relatively little authoritative case law on how this principle should be applied to consumer sales. Few cases are litigated, and even fewer are reported.

2.15 The time for acceptance may be suspended while the consumer is made to wait for information from the seller as to how an identified fault could best be put right,[19] or while goods are being repaired.[20] It may also be possible to reject after repairs have taken place, if the seller refuses to tell the consumer what was wrong with the goods, provided that the consumer made it clear before repair that he or she wanted to know what the fault was.[21] The buyer must stop using the goods once they are rejected.[22] At the point when the buyer rejects the goods, they become again the property of the seller.[23] The buyer does not, however, have to return the goods to the seller.[24]

Damages

2.16 Where goods are faulty, the buyer may be entitled to damages. Damages may be payable both where the buyer has rejected the goods,[25] and where the buyer has not rejected them.[26]

2.17 Generally, there are two types of loss for which a consumer buyer might seek compensation:

(1) *The difference in value.* Where the buyer keeps the goods, this is the difference between the value of the goods contracted for and the value of the goods actually received. Where the buyer has rejected the goods, it is the difference between the contract price and the current market price. If prices have increased since the original purchase, therefore, the buyer is entitled to extra compensation, in addition to a refund.

---

[19] *Clegg v Andersson (trading as Nordic Marine)* [2003] EWCA Civ 320; [2003] 1 All ER (Comm) 721.

[20] This is the result of SoGA, ss 35(6)(a) and 48D. See para 2.42, below.

[21] *J & H Ritchie Ltd v Lloyd Ltd* 2007 SC (HL) 89; [2007] 1 WLR 670; [2007] 2 All ER 353 was a commercial case, but should apply in the consumer context as well.

[22] At least, this is the traditional position. However, in *Lamarra v Capital Bank Plc* 2005 SLT (Sh Ct) 21 (affirmed by the Court of Session: 2007 SC 95) a driver drove a car for two months after seeking to reject, and the rejection was upheld. The point was not discussed by either the Sheriff Principal or the Court of Session.

[23] Scots common law provides that ownership of corporeal movables cannot pass without delivery (see Bell, *Commentaries on the Laws of Scotland* (5th ed 1826), Vol I, Book II, pp 166 to 169). Accordingly, although SoGA allows for ownership to pass without delivery from seller to buyer if, for example, goods were rejected by the buyer, redelivery to the seller would be necessary to revest title in the seller.

[24] SoGA, s 36.

[25] Above, s 51 allows the buyer to receive the difference between the contract price and the current market price.

[26] Above, ss 53 (for England) and 53A (for Scotland).

(2) *Any consequential losses*, including any injuries or damage to other property caused by the faulty products.

2.18 SoGA caters for both of these. The general contractual limits on foreseeable losses apply, so that consequential losses will only be recoverable if they were within the contemplation of the parties at the time of the sale.[27]

Burden of proof

2.19 The seller is only in breach of contract if the goods are defective at the time that they are delivered.[28] When a consumer uses the traditional UK remedies, the emergence of a fault at a later date is not, in itself, sufficient to establish that the goods were faulty when delivered.

2.20 Where the consumer is seeking to exercise their right to reject goods there will not normally be a problem in establishing that the fault existed when purchased; the short time period means that a court will generally accept that faults found upon inspection were present when the goods were delivered.

2.21 Where the consumer seeks damages, however, there may be problems. If a fault only becomes apparent after several months, it may be harder to persuade the court that the goods were defective when delivered.

Delivering the wrong quantity

2.22 SoGA contains specific provisions to deal with cases where the seller delivers the wrong quantity of goods.

2.23 Section 30(1) applies where too few goods are delivered. The buyer has two options:

(1) to reject the goods, recover the price paid and sue for any further loss; or

(2) to accept the goods that have been delivered and pay for them pro rata (although it is still possible to claim damages for breach).

2.24 Sub-sections 30(2) and (3) apply where an excess of goods is delivered. They give the buyer three options:

(1) to reject all the goods;

(2) to accept the correct amount and reject the rest; or

(3) to accept all the goods, paying for the extra goods at the contract rate.

---

[27] The general rule is derived from *Hadley v Baxendale* (1858) 9 Exch 341, which was a case concerning the sale of goods. See also SoGA, s 53 (for England) and s 53A (for Scotland).

[28] Although there is some confusion in case law: for example *Lexmead (Basingstoke) Ltd v Lewis* [1982] AC 225.

2.25   At first sight, these provisions appear to be generous to buyers, providing them with a range of options. However, these rights are subject to two qualifications. First, in English law, consumers may not reject the goods if the shortfall or excess is too small to be significant.[29] Secondly, if the buyer rejects the goods for a shortfall or excess, it appears that the seller may subsequently make delivery of the correct quantity within the delivery period.[30] Take an example where the seller undertakes to deliver a magnum of champagne to a consumer before their spouse's birthday on Saturday. If the seller delivers a standard bottle on Thursday, and the buyer rejects it, the seller may still make good the fault, and deliver the right quantity on Friday. However, by Saturday morning, the buyer is within their rights to reject the bottle and receive a full refund of the price. In Scots law, there is further statutory provision to the effect that the buyer is not entitled to reject the goods under s 30(1) or to reject the whole under s 30(2) unless the shortfall or excess, as appropriate, is material.[31]

2.26   The duty to deliver the correct quantity of goods may be thought of as an application of the more general duty to provide goods which correspond to their description.[32] Thus, where goods are not of the quantity described, the consumer may either reject the goods, or agree to accept a cure.

Late delivery

2.27   Consumers may only terminate a contract for late delivery if the delivery date is "of the essence of the contract" (in other words, in English law, a condition). Section 10 of SoGA states that this "depends on the terms of the contract". For example, if the buyer makes it clear that they want 50 bottles of wine only if they are delivered before the wedding, then the delivery date will be of the essence of the contract.

2.28   If no time is stipulated, section 29(3) of SoGA provides that delivery must be made within a "reasonable time". This is a question of fact and the court will take into account a broad range of factors. In Scots law, where a claim is based on non-delivery within a reasonable time (or on delivery after a time set out in the contract), the consumer has the right to retain the price in security for his claim for damages arising from the late delivery.[33]

2.29   In English law, if the delivery date is not a condition, it is likely to be construed as an "innominate term". This means that the consumer may terminate the contract if the delay is so prolonged that it deprives them of substantially the whole benefit they sought from the contract.[34] Otherwise, the buyer must accept a late delivery and sue for damages.

---

[29]   See *Shipton Anderson & Co v Weil Brothers & Co* [1912] 1 KB 574 and *Arcos Ltd v E A Ronaasen & Son* [1933] AC 470.

[30]   See *Benjamin's Sale of Goods* (7th ed 2006) para 8-052. Note that the seller could not agree to deliver the balance at a later time, as this would be an instalment delivery and, unless otherwise agreed, the buyer is entitled to receive all of the goods at the same time.

[31]   SoGA, s 30(2D) and (2E).

[32]   Under SoGA, s 13.

[33]   *Stair Memorial Encyclopaedia*, Vol 20, para 862.

[34]   See *Benjamin's Sale of Goods* (7th ed 2006) para 8-025.

THE CONSUMER SALES DIRECTIVE REMEDIES

2.30 In 2002, SoGA was amended to include new remedies for consumers.[35] The new Part 5A of SoGA gives consumers four new remedies, based on the 1999 Consumer Sales Directive (CSD).[36] The CSD is more concerned with ensuring the performance of the original contract than the traditional UK approach. Instead of allowing the buyer to end the contract and receive a refund, the emphasis is on allowing the seller to correct their defective performance.

2.31 The four European remedies are organised into two tiers. The first tier remedies allow for the repair or replacement of faulty goods. These are designed to be a consumer's primary remedy. If they fail, the consumer is allowed to rely on the second tier of rights: rescission or a reduction in price.

The first tier of rights: repair and replacement

2.32 In theory, the choice between repair and replacement is for the consumer, and the seller should honour that selection. In practice, however, the choice is often the seller's. The seller can refuse to carry out the chosen cure on the basis that it is impossible, or because it is disproportionate compared with the other remedies in the CSD.[37] This means that if a consumer buys a faulty washing machine which could easily be fixed, the consumer cannot demand a replacement washing machine. If both repair and replacement are disproportionate compared with the second tier remedies, then the consumer must accept a second tier remedy.[38]

2.33 Once the consumer has requested repair or replacement, and providing it is neither impossible nor disproportionate, the seller must carry out that remedy within a reasonable time and without significant inconvenience to the buyer. The seller must also bear any costs incurred in carrying out the remedy.[39]

The second tier of rights: rescission and reduction in price

2.34 Where repair and replacement are disproportionate, or where the seller has failed to carry out a cure within a reasonable time or without significant inconvenience, the consumer can rely on the secondary remedies of rescission or a reduction in the purchase price.[40]

---

[35] SoGA was amended by the Sale and Supply of Goods to Consumer Regulations 2002.

[36] Directive 1999/44/EC on certain aspects of the sale of consumer goods and associated guarantees, Official Journal L171 of 07.07.1999 p 12.

[37] SoGA, s 48B(3).

[38] It has been argued that this is out of line with the Directive, and too unfavourable to consumers.

[39] SoGA, s 48B(2).

[40] Above, s 48C.

2.35   Where the consumer opts to rescind the contract, the contract comes to an end in a similar way to the right to reject.[41] It appears that the consumer is not under an obligation to return the goods, and it should be sufficient to make them available to the seller.[42]

2.36   One major difference between rescission and the right to reject is that the buyer may be required to give some value for the use of the goods prior to rescission. If a consumer buys a car, which fails after one year, and the consumer rescinds the contract then the seller is entitled to a sum of money for one year's use of the car.[43] SoGA and the CSD do not define how this should be calculated. It is impossible to say with any confidence what the law is on this issue.[44]

2.37   In the case of rescission, the consumer returns the goods, and receives a refund with a discount for use. On the other hand, a reduction in the purchase price leaves the goods with the consumer but with a discount for their reduced value. The reduction in price is not defined, but should be "an appropriate amount".[45] It seems that the proper approach is to ask how much the consumer would have paid for the goods in their defective state. It will often be identical to the amount of damages payable under the traditional UK rules.

Burden of proof

2.38   A consumer seeking one of the CSD remedies receives the benefit of a six-month reverse burden of proof. This means that where a fault arises within the first six months after delivery there is a presumption that it existed at the time of delivery.[46] There are two ways to rebut the presumption. The seller may produce evidence that the fault did not exist at the time of delivery. Alternatively, the presumption may be incompatible with the nature of the goods or the nature of the fault.[47]

2.39   Following the expiration of the six-month period, the normal burden of proof applies, and it is up to the consumer to show that the goods were faulty at the time of delivery.

---

[41]   There is no statutory definition of "rescission" as used in SoGA, s 48C, and there is very little guidance as to how it should be used. It is, however, a term which is used in the Scots law of contract where the meaning is reasonably clear.

[42]   Again, this is not in the Act. *Benjamin's Sale of Goods* (7th ed 2006) para 12-097 says that "it may be assumed" that the same rule applies.

[43]   On the assumption that the consumer can prove that the car was faulty when purchased. See para 2.38, below, for more details on the burden of proof in consumer sales.

[44]   See para 8.150, below, for a discussion of the different possible calculations to be used.

[45]   SoGA, s 48C(1)(a).

[46]   Above, s 48A(3).

[47]   Above, s 48A(4).

THE INTERACTION BETWEEN THE TRADITIONAL REMEDIES AND THE DIRECTIVE REMEDIES

2.40 Generally speaking, the CSD remedies were inserted into SoGA as an additional layer of consumer protection, and there is little indication as to how the remedies are to interact. The consumer appears able to choose any of the remedies, providing the relevant requirements are met.

2.41 Some rules apply only to the CSD remedies. The most obvious example of this is the reverse burden of proof. There are other rules which are stated to apply only to the traditional remedies, but which are assumed to apply to the new remedies as well, such as the lack of an obligation to return goods to the seller following rejection.[48]

2.42 There is only one section of SoGA that attempts to tie the two regimes together. Section 48D states that the buyer who requires a repair or replacement must give the seller a reasonable time to carry out the remedy. A buyer cannot demand a repair or a replacement, and then change their mind and try to reject the goods. The seller must be given an opportunity to complete the repair or deliver the replacement.

PROCEDURE FOR BRINGING A CLAIM

2.43 If a consumer has rejected goods, but the seller refuses to refund the purchase price, the consumer needs to bring a claim to court. In England and Wales, the consumer will typically need to start a claim in the county courts by filling in a claim form (available online).[49]

2.44 In England and Wales, claims for low-value consumer goods will normally be allocated to the small claims track. This means that in most cases costs will not be awarded against the losing party. However, for claims worth over £5,000 the normal track is the fast track, where costs can be awarded, though some elements of costs are limited.[50] Where the claim is worth over £15,000 the winning party may be entitled to a higher amount in costs.[51]

---

[48] See para 2.15 above.

[49] http://www.moneyclaim.gov.uk.

[50] In particular, the winning party can only claim a fixed amount for the trial costs: see the Civil Procedure Rules, Part 46.

[51] The trial costs are not fixed for "multi-track" cases, unlike above.

2.45 In Scotland, claims may be brought under small claims procedure (claims up to £3000),[52] summary procedure (claims between £3,000 and £5,000)[53] or ordinary procedure (claims over £5,000).[54] As a general rule, court expenses are awarded to the party who succeeds in the claim.[55]

2.46 The delivery of faulty goods by the seller amounts to a breach of contract. The consumer, therefore, must submit any claim within the period allowed for breach of contract claims. In England and Wales, the relevant limitation period is six years from delivery.[56] In Scotland, there is a five-year period of prescription.[57]

CONTRACTS FOR THE SUPPLY OF GOODS, OTHER THAN SALES

2.47 As we have seen, UK law has long maintained a distinction between strict "sales" and other contracts for the supply of goods. SoGA only applies to sales, as narrowly interpreted.[58] Hire purchase contracts are covered by the Supply of Goods (Implied Terms) Act 1973, and other supply contracts by the Supply of Goods and Services Act 1982. Those Acts imply the same terms as to quality as SoGA implies into sales.

2.48 However, the remedies are different. As we discuss below, a buyer is not taken to have accepted goods after the lapse of a reasonable time. Instead, the buyer can only lose their right by a positive act, or inaction, once they are aware of the breach.

2.49 For hire and hire purchase contracts, there is an argument that following a breach the hirer is not entitled to a full refund of their payments. Instead, cases suggest that the hirer must pay for the use they have had from the goods and may only terminate for the future. A further complication is the way that the CSD applies to supply contracts other than sales, which we describe below.

[52] The Small Claims (Scotland) Order 1988, art 2, as amended by The Small Claims (Scotland) Amendment Order 2007, art 2(2). Forms for small claims procedure are available online.

[53] The Sheriff Courts (Scotland) Act 1971, s 35(1), as amended by The Sheriff Courts (Scotland) Act 1971 (Privative Jurisdiction and Summary Cause) Order 2007, art 3. Forms for summary procedure are available online.

[54] Ordinary procedure applies automatically where the above provisions for small claims and summary procedure do not apply.

[55] In Scotland, in small claims procedure, there is normally a limit on expenses based on the value of the claim; in summary procedure, expenses are decided on the basis of an approved table and, in ordinary procedure, expenses are subject to taxation (the process by which the court auditor determines how the expenses of the action are to be awarded).

[56] Limitation Act 1980, s 5.

[57] Prescription and Limitation (Scotland) Act 1973, s 6 and Schedule 1.

[58] See para 2.4, above.

Affirmation and waiver

2.50   The right to reject in sales contracts is a short term right that ceases after the buyer is deemed to have accepted the goods. By contrast, in other supply contracts, the right to terminate the contract is only lost through the consumer's conduct. In England and Wales, the right is lost only if the consumer "affirms" the contract, by recognising its continuing validity. The Law Commissions' 1987 Report set out the following principles of the law on affirmation:[59]

   (1)   On discovering the breach, an innocent party must elect between his available remedies.

   (2)   As a general rule, an innocent party cannot be held to have affirmed the contract, unless he had knowledge of the breach.[60]

   (3)   Affirmation may be express if the innocent party expressly refuses to accept the other party's repudiation of the contract.

   (4)   Affirmation may be implied if the innocent party does some act (for example, pressing for performance), from which it may be inferred that he recognises the continued existence of the contract.

   (5)   Mere inactivity by the innocent party after discovering the breach will not of itself constitute affirmation unless (a) the other party would be prejudiced by the delay in treating the contract as repudiated, or (b) the delay is of such length as to constitute evidence of a decision to affirm the contract.

   (6)   If the contract is held to be affirmed, the innocent party can no longer terminate the contract for breach.

2.51   In Scotland, in contracts for the supply of goods other than sales, the right to return the goods is lost where, through the consumer's conduct, the consumer is personally barred from insisting on the return of the goods. A buyer would be taken to have waived the breach if he has accepted the performance either expressly or by inference from the facts and circumstances of the case.[61]

2.52   The practical effect of the law in both jurisdictions is that a consumer may reject goods if a latent defect comes to light long after purchase. The consumer does not have to reject within the "reasonable period" set out in SoGA. The only time limit which applies is the limitation period under English law (six years), and the prescriptive period under Scots law (five years). Of course, the consumer would still have to prove that the fault existed at the time of delivery.

---

[59]   At para 2.51. For a more detailed discussion of various cases on the application of the affirmation doctrine to hire purchase contracts see K Mullan, "Satisfaction guaranteed or no deal" [1990] *Journal of Business Law* 231. The doctrine of affirmation has also been applied in a hire case: *Guarantee Trust of Jersey Ltd v Gardner* (1973) 117 SJ 564.

[60]   See *Yukong Line Ltd of Korea v Rendsberg Invesment Company of Liberia* [1996] 2 Lloyd's Rep 604 at 607.

[61]   See *Armia Ltd v Daejan Developments Ltd* 1979 SC (HL) 56; Sale and Supply of Goods (1987) Law Com No 160; Scot Law Com No 104, para 2.53; and E Reid, *Personal Bar* (2006) paras 3-08 (and following) and 3-42 (and following).

Hire and hire purchase contracts

2.53 For hire and hire purchase contracts, it is arguable that the breach of an implied condition only gives the innocent party a right to reject the goods and terminate[62] the contract for the future. It may not give the hirer an automatic right to recover all the money paid under the contract.

2.54 In England and Wales, the basic principle is set out in *Yeoman Credit*.[63] Here the defendant entered into an agreement for the hire purchase of a second-hand car which was so seriously defective that he was held to be entitled to reject it, terminate the contract and claim damages. However, because there had been no total failure of consideration he could not recover his deposit and the instalments he had paid.

2.55 In two subsequent hire purchase cases, however, the hirer was held to be entitled to reject goods and recover money paid under the contract despite obtaining some enjoyment from the goods. In *Charterhouse Credit v Tolly*[64] the hirer's use of a car was substantial and the parties conceded that there had not been a total failure of consideration. In this case, however, the hirer's damages consisted of the money he had paid under the contract less only a small deduction for use of the car. In *Farnworth Finance Facilities v Attryde*[65] a defective motorcycle had been driven for 4,000 miles. Despite such substantial use, the hirer recovered all the money he had paid under the contact. The Court of Appeal made no deduction for use because of the inconvenience he had suffered. There is therefore a degree of uncertainty about how to calculate damages when a consumer rejects goods under a hire purchase contract.

2.56 In Scotland, the Supply of Goods (Implied Terms) Act 1973 states that a breach by the creditor of any term of the hire-purchase agreement entitles the hirer to claim damages and, if the breach is material, to reject the goods and repudiate the contract.[66] Scottish courts would probably reach similar results to the English courts by applying principles of unjustified enrichment. For example, if a consumer repudiated the contract after enjoying three months effective use of the product, the courts would be unlikely to allow a full refund. On the other hand, if a product had caused trouble from the beginning, the consumer would probably get all their money back.

---

[62] Or, in Scots law, treat the contract as repudiated.

[63] *Yeoman Credit Ltd v Apps* [1962] 2 QB 508.

[64] [1963] 2 QB 683.

[65] [1970] 1 WLR 1053.

[66] S 12A.

The application of CSD remedies

2.57 Member states are required to apply CSD remedies for work and materials contracts.[67] The UK has therefore implemented CSD remedies by amending the 1982 Act in such a way as to extend CSD rights to work and materials contracts.[68]

2.58 The Directive does not apply to hire or hire purchase contracts, or to barter or exchange contracts.[69] In the case of hire or hire purchase contracts, the position is straightforward. The relevant legislation has not been amended, and CSD rights do not apply either to hire[70] or to hire purchase.[71]

2.59 For barter and exchange contracts, the position is more complex. The amendments to the 1982 Act applying to work and materials contracts also cover barter and exchange, suggesting that the CSD rights do apply. However, it has been argued that the Government may have exceeded its constitutional authority in amending the Act in this way.[72]

---

[67] In particular, art 1(4) specifically includes "contracts for the supply of consumer goods to be manufactured or produced" while art 2(5) applies the Directive where "installation forms part of the contract of sale… and the goods were installed by the seller or under his responsibility". For discussion of this point, see R Bradgate and C Twigg-Flesner, *Blackstone's Guide to Consumer Sales and Associated Guarantees* (2003) pp 22 to 26.

[68] Supply of Goods and Services Act 1982, ss 11M to 11S. It has been argued that these sections do not cover all the contracts within the CSD. It is possible that a contract (for example) to paint a portrait would be regarded as a service under UK law, but a sale under the CSD: see R Bradgate and C Twigg-Flesner, *Blackstone's Guide to Consumer Sales and Associated Guarantees* (2003), p 32.

[69] The CSD does not specifically define sales contracts, but we think that it must be interpreted in the light of the Draft Common Frame of Reference. This states, at p 341, that a sales contract is one in which the seller undertakes to transfer ownership of the goods to the buyer, for a price. R Bradgate and C Twigg-Flesner note that proposed amendments to include hire purchase, exchange or barter were specifically rejected by the Council: see *Blackstone's Guide to Consumer Sales and Associated Guarantees* (2003) pp 22 to 26.

[70] Note that s 11S of the Supply of Goods and Services Act 1982 does not apply to the implied terms relating to hire.

[71] See Supply of Goods (Implied Terms) Act 1973.

[72] R Bradgate and C Twigg-Flesner question whether the DTI had authority to use section 2(2) of the European Communities Act to amend primary legislation in respect of contracts not covered by the Directive: see *Blackstone's Guide to Consumer Sales and Associated Guarantees* (2003) p 10.

FLOWCHART OF REMEDIES FOR FAULTY GOODS

2.60 The flowchart on the next page lays out the scheme of remedies where a consumer has bought goods which turn out to be faulty. It only applies to "sales" under SoGA. We have tried to keep the chart as simple as possible, and it does not include all the complications which apply. For example, there is no reference to the fact that the right to reject can be revived after failed attempts to repair goods.

2.61 Even so, it can be seen that the remedies are quite complex for everyday transactions. It is no surprise, therefore, that our research into consumer knowledge of legal rights showed a general lack of awareness of consumer remedies for faulty goods.[73]

---

[73] See Appendix A.

REMEDIES FOR THE SALE OF FAULTY GOODS

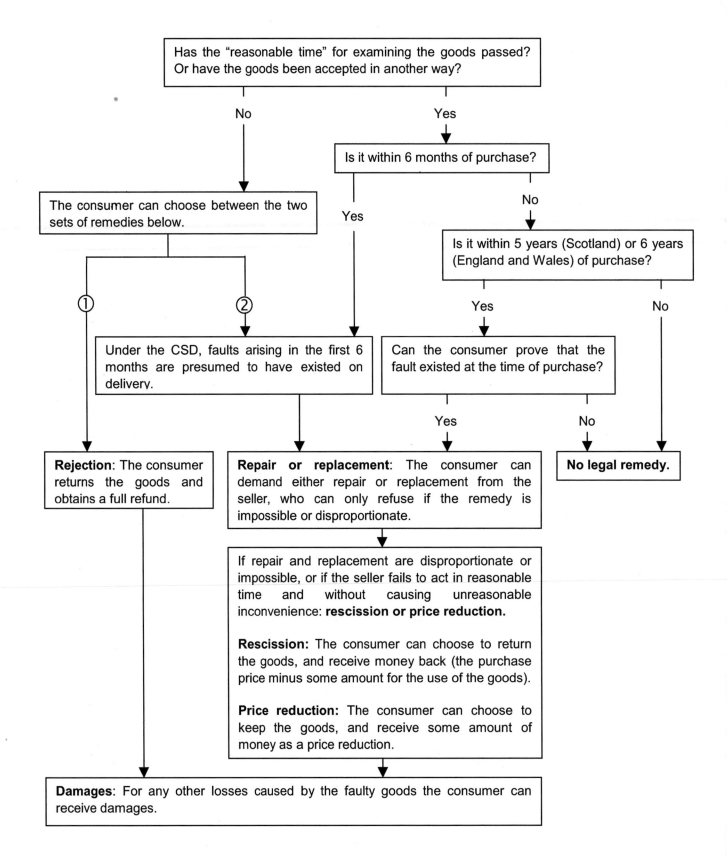

CANCELLATION RIGHTS FOR DISTANCE AND HOME SALES

2.62 EU directives provide consumers with specific rights to cancel contracts which were concluded away from the retailer's premises, either by distance selling methods or at the consumer's home. We have not considered these rights in the course of this project. However, it is necessary to be aware that these rights exist in order to understand the practical effect of the right to reject.

2.63 The Consumer Protection (Distance Selling) Regulations 2000 allow consumers a cancellation period of seven working days, starting the day after they receive the goods, during which they may cancel the contract for any reason and receive their money back. The Regulations apply where the trader's sales method relies solely on distance communication, such as post, internet or telephone sales.

2.64 The Cancellation of Contracts made in a Consumer's Home or Place of Work etc Regulations 2008 provide a cancellation period of seven calendar days, starting the day after the consumer is given notice of this right by the trader. During this period they may cancel the contract for any reason and receive their money back. These Regulations apply to contracts over £35 made at the consumer's home or place of work, at another person's home, or during an excursion organised by the trader away from its business premises. The most common example of this is what is known as "doorstep-selling".

2.65 The proposed directive on consumer rights, described below, would change these rights. The cancellation period would be increased to 14 calendar days, starting from the date of delivery in the case of distance selling and from the date the consumer signs the order form in the case of off-business premises selling.

THE EUROPEAN COMMISSION'S PROPOSAL FOR A DRAFT DIRECTIVE ON CONSUMER RIGHTS

2.66 On 8 October 2008 the European Commission published a proposal for a new directive on consumer rights, which would simplify four existing EU consumer rights directives into one set of rules.[74] The Commission proposed a "maximum harmonisation measure". This means that member states would not be able to provide greater rights in any area which fell within the scope of the proposed directive.

---

[74] COM (2008) 614/3: see http://ec.europa.eu/consumers/rights/cons_acquis_en.htm. It would replace not only the CSD but also directives on Unfair Contract Terms (93/13/EC); Distance Selling (97/7/EC) and Doorstep Selling (85/577/EC).

2.67   The proposed directive covers the remedies available where goods are not in conformity with the contract. It states that goods are presumed to be in conformity with the contract if they: comply with their description or sample; are fit for any particular purpose which the consumer made known to the trader; are fit for the purpose for which the goods are normally used; and[75] are of the quality which the consumer could normally expect.[76]

2.68   This clearly affects the issues contained in this Consultation Paper and it is important to set out how the proposed directive would change the current law in the areas considered by this paper. The main changes are as follows.

(1)   The right to reject would be removed from UK law. The available remedies would be those we have referred to as the CSD remedies: the first tier remedies of repair and replacement and the second tier remedies of rescission and reduction in price. For example, if a consumer buys a kettle in a shop, takes it home and finds that it does not work, the consumer would not be entitled to return it and receive a refund. Instead, the trader would be entitled to attempt a repair or replacement. The consumer would be entitled to rescind the contract if the repair or replacement could not be performed within a reasonable time or without significant inconvenience.

(2)   If the lack of conformity does not become apparent within two years, the consumer would lose the right to a remedy.[77] For example, if a consumer bought a steel joist which was then used in construction of their house and collapsed due to a defect after two and a half years, the consumer would not have enforceable contractual rights against the retailer. Currently, the law allows claims to be brought within six years in England and Wales, and, in Scotland, within five years from the date when the loss was, or could with reasonable diligence have been, discovered.

(3)   Rescission would not be allowed for minor defects.[78] For example, if a consumer bought a fridge, which on delivery had a scratch, their primary remedy would be a repair or replacement. If a repair was not possible and there was no available replacement, the question would arise whether the scratch was a minor defect. If so, then under the proposed directive, the consumer could not reject the fridge and would instead have to accept it for a reduced price.

---

[75]   The proposed directive uses "or" rather than "and", but we think this must be a mistake. Goods would only be in conformity with the contract if they comply with all four provisions. Goods are not in conformity, for example, just because they are fit for the purpose for which they are normally used if they do not comply with their description.

[76]   The proposed directive does not refer to other ways in which goods may not be in conformity with the contract, such as the requirement under SoGA, s 12 that the seller must have good title to the goods (providing the consumer with rights where the goods are stolen or subject to a finance agreement). It is not clear how far this would continue to be dealt with under national laws.

[77]   Art 28.

[78]   Art 26(3).

(4) Under the current CSD, it is the consumer who is entitled to choose between a repair or a replacement, providing that their choice is not impossible or disproportionate. The proposed directive allows the trader to choose between the two options.[79]

(5) Consumers would be permitted to move from a first to a second tier remedy where the trader had implicitly or explicitly refused to remedy the lack of conformity,[80] or where the same defect had reappeared more than once within a short period of time.[81]

(6) Where rescission is permitted, buyers would no longer be required to give some value for their use of the goods prior to rescission.[82]

(7) Consumers would have greater rights where goods are delivered late. Under the proposal, goods must be delivered on the agreed day, or if no time is agreed, within 30 days. If not, the consumer would be entitled to a full refund within seven days from the date of delivery.[83] This removes the current distinction between when time is, or is not, "of the essence".

(8) The specific provisions in UK law on delivering the wrong quantity would need to be repealed. Under the proposed directive, the consumer would not be entitled to reject the goods. Instead, the trader could attempt a repair or replacement (presumably by correcting their mistake).[84]

2.69 The proposed reduction in UK consumer rights would be greatest for those who buy from shops (either when they take goods home, or choose goods to be delivered later). With regard to distance sales, consumers would be able to return goods, whether faulty or not, provided they do so within 14 days of delivery. However, a consumer who buys an item from a shop, gets home, takes it out of the packet and finds that it is faulty would lose the right to ask for their money back. Instead, the trader would have a choice of offering a repair or replacement. The same would apply to distance sales of faulty goods where the consumer seeks to return the goods after 14 days. As we discuss in Part 3, this is a change from the principles underlying the Sale of Goods Act 1893 and subsequent legislation.

---

[79] Art 26(2).

[80] Art 26(4)(a).

[81] Art 26(4)(d).

[82] Recital 41.

[83] Art 22.

[84] The proposed directive provides relatively generous remedies for late delivery (a full refund) but much less generous remedies for a wrong delivery (where the goods are not as described, the trader may attempt a repair or replacement). There must come a point when the goods delivered are so different from the goods described that a wrong delivery should be regarded as no delivery (where, for example, the consumer ordered apples and receives oranges). The proposed directive gives little guidance on this issue.

PART 3
THE "RIGHT TO REJECT" IN UK LAW

INTRODUCTION

3.1 This Part considers the right to reject in more detail. We start with a description of the legislation, and then consider the case law.

3.2 The wording of the Sale of Goods Acts has proved to be extremely flexible. More or less the same provisions have been applied to grain in the nineteenth century and yachts in the twenty-first century. The flexibility of the factual approach to a "reasonable period" allows a great number of factors to influence the court, helping it to achieve a fair result in the individual case. However, this flexibility means that it is often not possible to predict whether the reasonable period has expired in a given case. The flexibility that has allowed the courts to develop the law can make it difficult for consumers to make a judgment about exercising their legal rights.

LEGISLATIVE PROVISIONS

3.3 The right to reject has a long history in English law, and was codified in the Sale of Goods Act 1893. Although we have used the phrase "the right to reject", that expression is not defined in the legislation. Under English common law, the breach of a term classified as a condition allows the buyer to terminate the contract. A breach of a term classified as a warranty does not allow the buyer to terminate the contract; the buyer is only entitled to damages.

3.4 The 1893 Act and Sale of Goods Act 1979 (SoGA) both classify the implied terms as to quality as conditions. The delivery of faulty goods, therefore, would ordinarily allow the buyer to return the goods and terminate the contract. However, the term will be treated as a mere warranty if the goods are accepted by the buyer.[1]

---

[1] Sale of Goods Act 1893, s 11(1)(c); SoGA, s 11(4).

3.5   In the Scots law of sale of goods, prior to the 1893 Act, the buyer's only remedy for the seller's breach of contract was rescission (restoration to the seller of his property and a refund of the price) and damages if appropriate.[2] Section 11(2) of the 1893 Act was drafted specifically for Scotland[3] and codified the common law in terms which gave the buyer a right to reject where there had been a material breach by the seller. The 1893 Act also effected a further change in Scots law by giving the buyer a general right to retain the goods and claim damages.[4]

3.6   In Scots law, there is nothing which parallels English law's classification of terms as "conditions" or "warranties". Instead, the right to reject is available when the seller's breach of contract is material.[5] However, for consumer sales, any breach by the seller of an express or implied term that goods are of satisfactory quality, or correspond to sample or description, is deemed to be material.[6] The concept of acceptance applies equally to Scotland.

The three methods of acceptance

3.7   The methods of acceptance are set out in section 35 of SoGA. The section states that the buyer is deemed to have accepted goods in three situations:

(1)   Where the buyer intimates to the seller that the goods have been accepted ("intimation"), provided he has had a reasonable opportunity to examine them.

(2)   Where the buyer does something with the goods which is inconsistent with the seller's ownership of the goods, provided he has had a reasonable opportunity to examine them ("inconsistent act").

(3)   Where, after the lapse of a reasonable time, the buyer retains the goods without telling the seller that the goods have been rejected ("the lapse of a reasonable time").

---

[2]   It was an exception to the general rule of the Scots common law that the primary remedy for breach of contract is to seek an order for implement, that is performance of the contract.

[3]   This was necessary as Scots law did not, and does not, distinguish between "conditions" and "warranties".

[4]   The general rule of the Scots common law of sale was that a buyer could not retain the item sold and claim damages: such a claim for damages (known, following Roman law, as the *actio quanti minoris*) was considered as a redrafting of the parties' contract. In contracts for the sale of goods limited exceptions to the general rule had been recognised prior to 1893, but the general right to retain the goods and claim damages was only confirmed in the 1893 Act.

[5]   SoGA, s 15B.

[6]   SoGA, s 15B(2).

3.8　These three methods were first set out in the Sale of Goods Act 1893.[7] However, the relevant section was substantially amended in 1994,[8] so that there are now sub-sections explaining when goods should, and should not, be deemed to have been accepted. One important point to note is that the concept of *a reasonable opportunity to examine the goods* is relevant to each of the three methods of acceptance.

3.9　We discuss the methods of acceptance in more detail below.

Method 1: Intimation of acceptance (section 35(1)(a) SoGA)

3.10　The goods will be regarded as accepted if the buyer intimates this to the seller, whether by words or by conduct. The Law Commissions' 1987 Report noted concerns about so-called "acceptance notes" where buyers were asked to sign an acknowledgement of receipt, including a clause to the effect that the goods were accepted, before there was an opportunity to inspect the goods.[9] The Report recommended an amendment, which was effected by the 1994 Act.[10] The position is now that a buyer will not be deemed to accept goods by intimation of acceptance unless they have had an opportunity to examine the goods.[11] Where the buyer is dealing as a consumer, the right to inspect cannot be waived by agreement.[12]

Method 2: Inconsistent acts (section 35(1)(b) SoGA)

3.11　A buyer will be considered to have accepted goods when he acts in a manner inconsistent with the seller's ownership, provided the buyer has had a reasonable opportunity to examine the goods. An example would be an act which makes it impossible to return the goods, such as putting paint on a wall.

3.12　The 1983 Consultation Paper[13] provisionally recommended that the "inconsistent act" rule of deemed acceptance should not apply to consumer sales, as the rule was too complex. However, that proposal was later reluctantly abandoned, and not recommended in the Report.[14]

The effect of agreeing to a repair: the 1994 reforms

3.13　The Law Commissions' 1987 Report identified a problem where a buyer agrees to have defects repaired, or requests a replacement. The concern was that this will be regarded as acceptance, and the buyer will thereby lose the right to reject. Such actions could either be considered inconsistent with the ownership of the seller, or an intimation of acceptance.

---

[7]　Sale of Goods Act 1893, s 35.

[8]　By the Sale and Supply of Goods Act 1994.

[9]　Sale and Supply of Goods (1987) Law Com No 160; Scot Law Com No 104, para 2.45.

[10]　Sale and Supply of Goods Act 1994.

[11]　SoGA, s 35(2).

[12]　Above, s 35(3).

[13]　Sale and Supply of Goods (1983) Law Com WP No 85; Scot Law Com CM No 58.

[14]　See Sale and Supply of Goods (1987) Law Com No 160; Scot Law Com No 104, p 51.

3.14   The Report recommended reform to address requests for repair and, also, where the buyer disposes of an item by, for example, giving it to someone else. These recommendations were adopted in the 1994 Act, which inserted the following subsection into section 35 of SoGA:

> (6) The buyer is not by virtue of this section deemed to have accepted the goods merely because –
>
>> (a) he asks for, or agrees to, their repair by or under an arrangement with the seller; or
>>
>> (b) the goods are delivered to another under a sub-sale or other disposition.

3.15   It is important to emphasise that the amendment means that a request for cure, *of itself*, will not be regarded as acceptance. It does not preclude the possibility that, in all the circumstances, the buyer might be considered to have accepted, where he has, among other things, requested repair.

3.16   It is also worth noting that subsection 6(a) only applies to agreements *with the seller* to repair the goods. If the buyer makes repair arrangements with a third party, for example the *manufacturer* of the washing machine, then subsection 6(a) will not provide a shield against a claim that this amounts to acceptance.

Method 3: Lapse of time (section 35(4) SoGA)

3.17   Buyers are regarded as having accepted goods if they retain them after a reasonable time without intimating to the seller that they have rejected them. This is now contained in section 35(4):

> (4) The buyer is also deemed to have accepted the goods when, after the lapse of a reasonable time he retains the goods without intimating to the seller that he has rejected them.

3.18   Section 59 states that the question of what constitutes a reasonable time is one of fact. The 1987 Report considered whether this method of acceptance should also be subject to the proviso that the buyer should have a reasonable opportunity to examine the goods. No change was recommended. However, the 1994 Act did introduce a new subsection (5), which provides:

> (5) The questions that are material for determining for the purposes of subsection (4) above whether a reasonable time has elapsed include whether the buyer has had a reasonable opportunity of examining the goods for the purposes mentioned in subsection (2) above.

3.19   Thus it is possible for goods to be accepted due to lapse of time even though there has not been a reasonable opportunity to examine, although this is a factor to consider when assessing reasonableness.

THE CASE LAW

3.20 Although the right to reject has a long history, it has generated relatively few cases. We discuss those cases which help provide guidance, though some were decided under previous statutes,[15] and some are commercial in nature. The law on acceptance does not, in most instances, differ between commercial parties and consumers: both rely on section 35. However, the factual circumstances may be different.

Early cases

3.21 Under the 1893 Act, in England and Wales, a buyer could not usually reject goods where the contract was for the sale of *specific goods*. The paradigm situation would have been where a buyer agreed to buy a horse from a seller, after taking a look at the horse. Here, the guiding principle was "buyer beware".

3.22 However, buyers were entitled to reject *non-specific goods*. Here the sale only bound the buyer after the buyer had had an opportunity to examine the goods. That said, the early cases suggest that the buyer should inspect the goods immediately, at the place of delivery. In *Perkins v Bell*,[16] for example, the seller delivered barley to the buyer at a railway station. The buyer then sent it to a brewer, who rejected it. The Court of Appeal said that the buyer should have inspected the barley at the station, before property passed.[17]

3.23 Slowly, over the years, the courts started to relax the rules to allow more time to inspect goods. By the mid-twentieth century, the courts no longer required inspection to take place before property passed to the buyer. Instead, there was a period in which property conditionally passed, during which the buyers could inspect the goods.[18]

---

[15] There is some debate whether old cases are relevant in considering the law as it now stands: see P S Atiyah, J N Adams and H MacQueen, *The Sale of Goods* (11th ed 2005) chapter 1. Furthermore, several of the cases cited were decided before the 1994 amendments to SoGA.

[16] [1893] 1 QB 193.

[17] However, this was not always applied strictly. For example, in *Grimoldby v Wells* (1875) LR 10 CP 391, the buyer lived nine miles away from the seller. The goods were driven halfway by the seller, where they were put onto the buyer's cart. It was held that the buyer was entitled to examine the goods in his own barn. Furthermore, Scots law appears to have been much less strict than English law on the question of the examination of goods. See Bell, *Commentaries on the Laws of Scotland* (5th ed 1826), Vol I, Book III, p 439.

[18] *Kwei Tek Chao v British Traders and Shippers Ltd* [1954] 2 QB 459 at 487 by Devlin J.

3.24 The extent of the change in attitude is illustrated by a 1979 commercial case, decided under the 1893 Act. In *Manifatture Tessile Laniera Wooltex v J B Ashley Limited*[19] the seller sold significant quantities of cloth to the buyer, in various batches. The buyers resold the cloth to sub-buyers without examining it, and seven weeks after the first delivery, began to receive complaints from the sub-buyers. Following some meetings between the sellers and buyers, and threats from the sellers that rejection would be treated as a breach of contract, the buyers sought to reject the goods three and a half months after the initial delivery. The Court of Appeal held that the buyers were entitled to reject, and that the reasonable time had not elapsed.

The *Bernstein* case

3.25 It remained to be seen how far these commercial principles would apply to consumers. In *Bernstein v Pamson Motors (Golders Green) Limited*[20] the consumer bought a new car on 7 December 1984, for £8,000. It broke down on 3 January 1985, after having been driven for 140 miles, and the buyer sought to reject it the following day.

3.26 Mr Justice Rougier accepted that in the context of cars, purchasers are entitled to try the car out generally, but came to the conclusion that the use of a car for some three weeks and 140 miles did constitute a reasonable time to examine the car. The period had expired, even though the judge was willing to discount a period during which the buyer had been ill.

3.27 Whilst it seems that Mr Justice Rougier was adopting an objective view of "reasonable time", he specifically discounted the period of illness, noting that it was reasonable to take account of the buyer's position as well as that of the seller. However, the discounting of the period of illness seems somewhat inconsistent with the general objective view that Mr Justice Rougier was espousing.

3.28 Mr Justice Rougier was clear that the kind of defect arising does not affect the length of the reasonable time. Whether the defect is easy to discover or difficult, the same time period should apply; this encourages finality in the transaction, and enables the seller to "close his ledger" after a short period of time.[21] In other words, even if the fault could not possibly have been discovered before the end of the reasonable time, the right to reject the goods may well have been lost.

Is Bernstein good law?

3.29 There are considerable doubts as to whether *Bernstein* was correctly decided. An appeal was launched, but the case was settled and the appeal was never heard.

---

[19] [1979] 2 Lloyd's Reports 28.

[20] [1987] 2 All ER 220.

[21] *Bernstein v Pamson Motors (Golders Green) Limited* [1987] 2 All ER 220 at 230.

3.30   Just a few days after the *Bernstein* decision, the Court of Appeal adopted a more generous approach to rejection in a case which appeared to contradict *Bernstein*. In *Rogers v Parish (Scarborough) Limited*[22] the purchaser of a £14,000 car had problems from the moment of delivery until he sought to reject it over six months later. During that time the car had been safe enough to drive, and the buyer had driven over 5,500 miles. Also during that time, there had been a number of attempted repairs by the sellers, none of which managed to cure the problems. The Court of Appeal agreed with the purchaser that the car was not of merchantable quality,[23] and that he had been entitled to reject it.

3.31   On first sight, this case appears to allow for a long period of rejection, but the Court of Appeal did not rule on that point. The sellers had not argued the point in the High Court, and only tried to argue it when the case reached the appeal stage. Such arguments were not allowed by their Lordships, and so the point was not explored.

3.32   Even if *Bernstein* was correct at the time, Professor Goode argues that it would not be decided the same way after the 1994 amendments and the insertion of subsections 35(5) and (6) into SoGA.[24] This position has also been taken by the Court of Appeal in *Clegg v Andersson T/A Nordic Marine*.[25] Sir Andrew Morritt VC said:

> It is unnecessary to express a view as to whether the decision of Mr Justice Rougier was correct before the amendment effected by the Sale and Supply of Goods Act, 1994. In my view it does not represent the law now.[26]

The *Clegg* case

3.33   *Clegg* involved a £236,000 yacht that was delivered in August 2000 with a keel that was substantially heavier than it should have been. The buyer used the yacht on a number of occasions, but was in regular contact with the sellers about how the problem should be remedied. The buyer sought information about the best way to proceed, and he did not receive plans until 15 February 2001. Three weeks later the buyer sought to reject the yacht and receive back the purchase price.

3.34   Though the buyer's case was dismissed in the High Court, the Court of Appeal held that he had been entitled to reject the yacht. Sir Andrew Morritt VC stated:

> In the light of the undisputed fact that Mr Clegg did not receive the information he had sought in August and September 2000 until 15 February 2001 I consider the three weeks which elapsed thereafter until the letter of rejection dated 6 March 2001 did not exceed a reasonable time.

---

[22] [1987] QB 933.

[23] This was the phrase used in the pre-1994 legislation.

[24] R Goode, *Commercial Law* (3rd ed 2004) p 355.

[25] [2003] EWCA Civ 320; [2003] 1 All ER (Comm) 721.

[26] Above, at [63].

3.35   Though three weeks had been considered too long in *Bernstein*, the Court of Appeal in *Clegg* thought that it was not too long. The 1994 amendments, by making the time for examination only one issue relevant to the reasonable time for rejection, convinced the court that a longer time period could be permissible.

3.36   There was no indication in *Clegg* as to when the reasonable period would have expired. The Court may have envisaged quite a long period:

> Amendments made in the 1994 Act were designed to strengthen the buyer's right to reject by restricting the circumstances in which he might be held to have lost it.[27]

3.37   Professor Reynolds interprets *Clegg* as a move away from the "harsh objective approach" of *Bernstein* towards a more subjective approach, taking into account the particular facts between the particular parties.[28]

The *Truk* case

3.38   *Truk (UK) Limited v Tokmakidis GmbH*[29] involved a commercial party that sought to reject equipment fitted to its vehicle.[30] The buyer had only discovered the non-conformity of the equipment almost six months after it had been delivered. There then followed negotiations between the parties which lasted for over six months before the buyer rejected the goods.

3.39   Judge Raymond Jack QC held that the buyer was entitled to reject the goods, even though this took place over a year after the sale. He set out five factors which should be taken into account when calculating the reasonable period:

(1)   The reasonable period is the time in which it is reasonable to intimate rejection, bearing in mind both the buyer's and the seller's position.

(2)   The reasonable time to intimate acceptance is not less than the time required to examine the goods.

(3)   The reasonable time may be longer than the time required to examine the goods.

(4)   Dealings between the parties may extend the reasonable time.

(5)   Where faults are likely to be latent, a longer time period may be reasonable to permit a period of use in which the faults may appear.[31]

---

[27]   Above, at [74] by Hale LJ.

[28]   F Reynolds, "Loss of the Right to Reject" (2003) 119 *Law Quarterly Review* 544.

[29]   [2000] 2 All ER (Comm) 594.

[30]   Judge Raymond Jack QC concluded that the contract was for the sale of goods: above at 601.

[31]   Above at 604.

3.40 In this case, the fact that the vehicle was sold with the intention that it should be resold was important. The reasonable period was said to take into account the amount of time it was likely to take to find a sub-buyer, and a period for that sub-buyer to test out the goods. Six months was appropriate in this case, whereas a vehicle which was not intended to be resold could be retained for one or two months before acceptance would be deemed to have taken place.[32]

3.41 Once the faults had been discovered, the judge held that the buyer was entitled to enter into negotiations over the proper course of action, and the time taken in this case was regarded as reasonable. One element that the judge focused on was the fact that the buyer had refused to pay when asked; this showed the buyer had reserved its position pending further investigations.[33]

The *Bowes* case

3.42 In *Bowes v Richardson & Son Ltd*,[34] a county court allowed rejection after seven months. Here a consumer bought a new car. There were many problems with it, some of which occurred immediately after its delivery and others that did not become apparent for several months. The seller carried out repairs. However, seven months after delivery, the AA inspected the car and found continuing problems, showing that the seller had never fully repaired it. The buyer then attempted to reject the car. The court had to determine whether the car had been accepted by lapse of a reasonable time.

3.43 The court followed the approach in *Clegg* and decided that the buyer was entitled to reject the goods. It reasoned that if goods are repaired, a buyer should have a reasonable period of time to assess the effectiveness of the repairs. As the car in this case was never fully repaired, the buyer did not have the opportunity to assess the repairs and cannot be said to have ever accepted the goods. The court also said that section 35(6) of SoGA meant that the buyer did not lose the right to reject the goods through agreeing to allow the seller to repair the goods. However, this decision was based entirely on the facts and being only a county court decision it is unclear whether a similar approach would be taken in future cases.

The *Jones* case

3.44 In *Jones v Gallagher* the Court of Appeal took a more restrictive approach.[35] The couple in *Jones* had their kitchen installed at the end of April 2000, and subsequently made some complaints to the kitchen fitter. They complained about several matters, including the colour of the kitchen, and some remedial work was done. After the repairs the couple made further complaints, though not about the colour. On 27 September 2000 the couple told the fitters that they would strip out the kitchen and proceedings were begun on 9 October. The judge at first instance held that the couple had accepted the kitchen and the Court of Appeal agreed.

---

[32] Above at 605.

[33] Above at 606.

[34] *Bowes v Richardson & Son Limited*, 28 January 2004 (unreported).

[35] *Jones v Gallagher (trading as Gallery Kitchens and Bathrooms)* [2004] EWCA Civ 10; [2005] 1 Lloyd's Reports 377.

3.45 Key to the court's decision seems to have been the fact that section 59 of SoGA states that the question of what is a reasonable time is one of fact.[36] It was decided that there was sufficient evidence in the case to support the judge's conclusion, so the appeal could not succeed.[37] More generally, Lord Justice Buxton referred to the judgment in *Clegg* but denied that it laid down a rule that time did not run during a period of complaint and request for rectification. In his view, the purpose of the 1994 Act was not to lay down such a rule, but merely to correct what had previously been thought; that the right to reject was lost automatically if the buyer engaged in discussion or activity about repair. Any delay due to repairs and such like was merely a factor to be taken into account when assessing what was the reasonable time. Lord Justice Thomas took a similar line, emphasising that hard and fast rules would fetter the discretion of the judge to decide what a reasonable time was, which, as section 59 provides, is a question of fact.

3.46 The *Jones* decision is itself open to criticism. The Court of Appeal seems to have overlooked the fact that acceptance within the meaning of SoGA was irrelevant. The transaction in *Jones* was not one of sale – it was a contract for work and materials. This was implicitly acknowledged by the court at first instance, since they referred to the terms implied by section 3(2) of the Supply of Goods and Services Act 1982 which applies to transfers of goods which are not sales.[38] SoGA and the 1982 Act are mutually exclusive in their scope. This fact throws doubt on the validity of the decision in *Jones* as a whole. The court should in fact have considered whether the contract for work and materials had been *affirmed*. This is not the same as the statutory concept of acceptance within SoGA.[39]

The *Ritchie* case: lack of information and the right to reject

3.47 In *J & H Ritchie Limited v Lloyd Limited*[40] the House of Lords, hearing an appeal from Scotland, considered a dispute relating to a combination seed drill and harrow. The harrow had vibrated when first used and the seller arranged to repair it, while supplying the buyer with a replacement machine. The seller repaired the harrow, as the sheriff principal found, to "factory gate standard", but refused to tell the buyer what had been wrong with it. The buyer discovered, through informal means, that the harrow had been missing some bearings when originally constructed. The buyer was concerned that the effect of operating the harrow without the bearings could mean that other problems had been created, and decided to reject the harrow.

---

[36] Above, at [16].

[37] Above, at [27].

[38] Supply of Goods and Services Act 1982, s 1(2)(a).

[39] Discussed above at paras 3.7 to 3.19.

[40] 2007 SC (HL) 89; [2007] 1 WLR 670; [2007] 2 All ER 353.

3.48 The House of Lords held that the buyers had been entitled to reject the harrow, overturning the decision of the Inner House of the Court of Session. Their Lordships reached this decision through agreeing that a term should be implied into the parties' contract which required the seller to inform the buyer as to the nature of the repairs that had been carried out. The decision has been the subject of considerable debate as differing reasoning was used by their Lordships.[41]

3.49 The two main strands of reasoning were those of Lord Hope and of Lord Rodger. Lord Hope said that this term should be implied into the original contract of sale between the parties given the facts of this particular case. Lord Rodger however reasoned that there was a separate contract for repair between the two parties and that the term should be implied as part of the latter contract. There are difficulties with both approaches and it is not clear what factors may lead to the implication of such a term in either case.[42]

3.50 As Professor Thomson points out, the approach taken in *Ritchie* was based on the particular facts of the case, which will inevitably lead to more litigation on the issue of when a buyer retains a right to reject goods during or after repair.[43] The decision would appear too complex for consumers, advisers or retail staff to apply in practice. The House of Lords was grappling with an important issue: what rights does a buyer have when the retailer acts unreasonably in the process of repairing goods by, for example, not providing information? However, the case does not provide a practical answer. We discuss reform of this issue in Part 8.

3.51 The *Ritchie* case also raised the question of what happens to a buyer's right to reject goods when, by agreement, the seller carries out repairs. Section 35(6) of SoGA states that if a buyer asks for, or agrees to, repairs being carried out by a seller, they are not said to have accepted the goods and therefore retain the right to reject. SoGA does not, however, define when or how a buyer can exercise this right to reject whilst repairs are being carried out or after they have been completed.

---

[41] See J M Thomson, "A Simple Case? – J & H Ritchie Ltd v Lloyd Ltd, 2007 SLT 377" 2007 *JR* 241; V Mak, "The seller's right to cure defective performance – a reappraisal" 3 *Lloyd's Maritime and Commercial Law Quarterly* (2007) 409; D Carr, "Repairs, Refusals and Rejections" [2007] *Cambridge Law Journal* 498; P Hood, "'A Stitch in Time'? Repairs and Rejection in Sale of Goods" 2008 *Edinburgh Law Review* 316; K C F Loi, "Sale of goods in Scotland – repairing defects in the law" [2007] *Journal of Business Law* 807; and K F K Low, "Repair, rejection & rescission: an uneasy solution" (2007) 123 *Law Quarterly Review* 536.

[42] K C F Loi suggests that there is a strict test for implying terms on the facts of a case, and that there was insufficient evidence in this case. It is argued that the term implied was neither necessary to give the agreement "business efficacy" nor the kind of term that both parties would have agreed to if questioned by an "officious bystander": "Sale of goods in Scotland – repairing defects in the law: J&H Ritchie Ltd v Lloyd Ltd" [2007] *Journal of Business Law* 807.

[43] J M Thomson, "A Simple Case? – J & H Ritchie Ltd v Lloyd Ltd" 2007 *JR* 241 at 246.

3.52   Professor Thomson puts forward two possible interpretations. The first is that the buyer retains the right to reject during the course of repairs and after repairs have been completed, even if the repairs have been successful. The second is that if after repair the goods are no longer defective and therefore conform to the contract, the buyer loses the right to reject.[44] As *Ritchie* was decided on the basis of an implied term requiring the seller to provide the buyer with full information, the House of Lords found it unnecessary to decide which of these interpretations is correct. Lord Hope's opinion does, however, tend to favour the second one:

> It may then be said that a buyer who, having been equipped with all that knowledge, allows the seller to incur the expense of repair is under an implied obligation to accept and pay for the goods once the repair has been carried out.[45]

This suggests that the right to reject is suspended while the repair is carried out and is lost following a successful repair.

CONCLUSION

3.53   It appears that the reasonable period for examination, which is relevant to each of the three methods of acceptance, is not generally possible to calculate in advance with any accuracy. Even the courts appear to struggle with the assessment.

3.54   The law has developed in line with the increasing complexity of goods. With respect to simple goods in the nineteenth century the period deemed reasonable for examination was very short, whereas modern complicated goods necessarily attract a longer period.

3.55   *Bernstein* seemed to lay down a somewhat harsh objective rule, which did not take into account the specific defect. The case emphasised the need for a seller to be able to "close his ledger", but then confusingly took into account factors such as the buyer's illness. However, it has been argued that *Bernstein* is no longer good law today, after the amendments made by the 1994 Act.

3.56   What is the state of the law today? It seems that the courts would allow longer than the three week interpretation of "a reasonable time" in *Bernstein*. Beyond this more general observation, it is difficult to lay down clear rules.

---

[44]   Above, at 243 to 244.

[45]   *J & H Ritchie Limited v Lloyd Limited* 2007 SC (HL) 89; [2007] 1 WLR 670; [2007] 2 All ER 353 at [15] by Lord Hope.

3.57   Furthermore, the status of periods of negotiation and repair is complicated by the tension between the decisions in *Clegg* and *Jones*. Bradgate describes *Jones* as casting doubt on the apparent clarification in *Clegg* and having the effect of "resurrecting uncertainty about whether a buyer who requests or agrees to repair may nevertheless be held to have accepted the goods by lapse of time during the period taken to effect repair."[46] Given the confusion in *Jones* about the nature of the transaction, it might be thought that *Clegg* is to be preferred. However, the facts in *Clegg* were unusual. The defect was noticed immediately, and the key information was not supplied for some time.

3.58   To conclude, it is not possible to say with a sufficient degree of certainty how long the reasonable period for examination is because it depends upon the facts of the case. In a standard case, a consumer may have sought a number of repairs, and these may have been unsuccessful. The interplay between the repairs and the period for rejection is difficult, and it means that a buyer attempting to exercise the right to reject will face difficult judgments.

3.59   Consumer Direct is a government-funded telephone and online service offering information and advice on consumer issues. It has reported that consumers often face difficulties when seeking to reject faulty goods beyond a two week period due to ambiguity as to what constitutes a reasonable period. This suggests that the effect of the uncertainty, in practical terms, may be that consumers find it difficult to reject faulty goods after two weeks, when legally the period for rejection is probably longer.

---

[46]   R Bradgate, "Remedying the Unfit Fitted Kitchen" (2004) 120 *Law Quarterly Review* 558 at 562.

PART 4
CONSUMERS' VIEWS: A SUMMARY OF THE FDS RESEARCH

INTRODUCTION

4.1 As part of this project, we commissioned FDS International Limited (FDS) to research consumers' perceptions of their legal rights when they buy faulty goods. In February 2008, FDS ran eight focus groups, and one mini-focus group, in which participants were asked about their views on consumer rights. The discussion revolved around a number of scenarios involving faulty goods.

4.2 FDS collected and analysed the evidence, and produced a report, which is attached as Appendix A to this Consultation Paper. Below is a summary of that report, drawing out some of the conclusions which are of greatest importance for our project.

LACK OF AWARENESS OF CONSUMER LEGAL RIGHTS

4.3 The most striking finding of the research was the extent to which participants were unaware of their legal rights. This was illustrated by reactions to the phrase "this does not affect your statutory rights". Participants were familiar with the words, but almost universally unaware as to what their rights were. Some participants had no comprehension of what the words meant; some had mistaken comprehensions; others said:

It means your rights as a consumer but you don't know what they are.

4.4 Participants had a flawed understanding of their legal rights. Some mistakenly believed they had a good understanding of the law, whilst others freely admitted their lack of knowledge. Some consumers underestimated their legal rights whilst others overestimated their legal rights.

4.5 Participants' lack of knowledge was also illustrated by their perceptions of how long rights last:

(1) Participants believed that they had a legal right to a full refund for 30 days (two-thirds of responses) or for one year (one-third of responses). Virtually no one was aware that they must reject goods within a "reasonable period".

(2) One-third of people thought that the right to a replacement lasted for 30 days, whilst one-half believed that it lasted for one year. A few participants chose a different period, but it appeared that no one identified the six-month reverse burden of proof.

(3) Participants tended to think that they had a longer right to repairs, with most answers stating that it lasted for one year (one-half) or that it depended on the guarantee (one-third).

THE RIGHT TO REJECT

4.6　In one scenario, participants were asked whether they would accept a replacement where low-value goods turned out to be faulty. The scenario involved a kettle with a faulty element. Most people said that they would be happy to accept a replacement, but a significant minority of participants (20%) said that they would not, and would demand a refund, or a different product. Their confidence in the product would have been lost, and they would fear a recurrence of the same fault in a replacement which would cause further inconvenience.

4.7　The research indicates that there are some faults which are more likely to cause consumers to request a refund, rather than a repair or replacement. For example, faults which are potentially dangerous can destroy confidence in a brand and model, so that consumers think they should receive a refund rather than a repair or replacement. In addition, certain other faults incline consumers to think that the same fault will recur in replacements, such as poor stitching in clothing.

4.8　People are more likely to accept a replacement if they had made a considered decision to purchase a particular model or brand in the first place. If the faulty item is a well-known brand, a distinctive model or a highly priced product, they are more likely to accept a replacement, believing the fault to be a one-off incident, and being keen to have the product they carefully selected. Conversely, if they had made a less considered decision, the brand is less well-known, or the product is cheaper, they are more likely to expect faults to recur in any replacement, and want their money back or a credit note so that they can buy a different product.

4.9　Most participants objected to the suggestion that the right to reject might be abolished. They felt that it was appropriate that it was one of the options available to consumers who purchased faulty goods. Most people were aware that they had a right to reject goods, even though they might not necessarily rely on it.

4.10　When considering the faulty new car scenario, as an example of a high value complex item, it appeared that participants were willing to accommodate retailers by giving them a chance to put the fault right, especially where the fault was cosmetic or minor. Most consumers recognised that rejecting a new car for a minor fault would be disproportionate. Participants were also influenced by manufacturers' warranties and guarantees rather than their understanding of the law. However, if the fault was potentially dangerous, participants would generally prefer to receive a replacement car; or if they had lost confidence in the model, a refund.

4.11　With the washing machine scenario, given the relatively high price and the potential inconvenience of getting a replacement, participants tended to expect the retailer to arrange a repair when possible.

4.12　When the "reasonable period" for rejection was explained, some participants could see the benefits of flexibility, and listed a number of factors which they thought should affect the length of the time period. However, it appeared that not everyone agreed as to what was "reasonable". Some thought that 30 days was adequate while others argued for a longer period.

4.13 Though many people could see the benefits of a flexible time period, the option of standardising the time for rejection was more popular than the possibility of abolition.

4.14 In certain situations many participants felt strongly that they should be able to reject goods, for a full refund. In particular, people stated that they should be able to get a full refund where a replacement or repair had failed. Where a product failed twice, participants said that they would no longer trust the product.

4.15 When asked to consider the Christmas gift scenario, where there was an extended delay between purchasing and examining goods, almost all participants said that consumers should be entitled to a refund.

THE CSD REMEDIES

Repair and replacement

4.16 In general, people seemed comfortable with the concepts of repair and replacement, though their perception of their legal rights appeared to have been influenced by commercial guarantees.

4.17 Repairs were seen to be more relevant for high value items, such as cars, washing machines and other white goods. Repairs were thought to be unlikely to be offered in the case of low value goods where the labour costs involved might exceed the price of the product.

4.18 Participants were questioned about how long it was reasonable to wait for repairs. People wanted repairs to be carried out quickly, especially on important products such as washing machines which might be used almost every day. Some thought that repairs should be carried out in a day (though three days might be acceptable in some situations) whereas other participants (without families) might be prepared to accept a longer period.

4.19 Participants would generally only be prepared to accept one replacement. If that replacement proved unsatisfactory, they would expect to receive a refund.

Reduction in price and rescission

4.20 Whilst the first tier remedies were familiar to consumers, the second tier remedies of reduction in price and rescission came across as "strange" and "alien". Rescission is not a word people understand. Nor did consumers think it appropriate for a retailer to offer less than a full refund when a product was returned. It was seen as simply unfair: if the product was faulty the consumer should not lose part of the purchase price. Further, some participants thought that the law should go the other way - the consumer should be compensated if they have been inconvenienced.

4.21 Participants were presented with two scenarios that posed the possibility of keeping a product with a cosmetic or minor fault in return for a price reduction. Very few participants recognised this as a legal right. This remedy was only seen as appropriate in limited situations, such as where white goods or furniture suffered minor damage upon delivery. If the damage was not normally visible, a consumer might be willing to accept an item at a reduced price as an alternative to the inconvenience of having the item taken away and a replacement item delivered. In general, however, people wanted fully functional goods and would not be interested in a reduction in the price.

OTHER FINDINGS

4.22 Consumers were highly influenced by the policies set out by retailers and manufacturers. Participants also thought that market reputations would help them when they faced a problem. In their opinion, the second tier remedy of rescission with partial refund was unlikely to be used, as it would damage a retailer's reputation. In parallel, many participants said that one of the reasons for choosing a shop is that shop's returns policy.

4.23 Consumers may benefit from retailers' efforts to retain their goodwill. However, they may also accept what a retailer tells them their policy is, even if this is less generous to the consumers than their legal rights.

4.24 It appears from our research that retailers' and manufacturers' guarantees influence consumers' views of their rights. In some situations they encourage a belief that remedies can last for a long time, such as those who thought that they can get a refund for faulty products for a full year. On the other hand, some shops' policies may have led some consumers to underestimate their rights, for example to believe that all consumer rights are limited to 30 days.

4.25 Participants suggested that consumer rights should be publicised and that key rights should be posted in prominent positions in stores.

PART 5
A SUMMARY OF OTHER EMPIRICAL RESEARCH

5.1 In this Part we summarise four other empirical studies which have looked at perceptions and use of legal remedies for faulty goods.

OFFICE OF FAIR TRADING REPORT ON CONSUMER DETRIMENT (APRIL 2008)[1]

5.2 The Office of Fair Trading (OFT) report on consumer detriment assessed the frequency and impact of consumer problems with goods and services in Britain. The findings were based upon a survey, the key objectives of which were to measure the overall value of detriment in the economy and examine complaints behaviour. The survey covered the full range of goods and services, including many which do not fall within the scope of our project, such as personal banking services and insurance.

5.3 Respondents were asked to identify any problems they had experienced for which they had a genuine cause for complaint. Using this definition, around a third of respondents (34%) reported one problem or more in the last 12 months with goods or services they had purchased, with 542 problems identified in the survey for every 1000 people interviewed. When projected across the overall UK population, this leads to an estimated 26.5 million problems over a 12 month period.

5.4 Consumer detriment in the UK economy amounted to an estimated £6.6 billion over a 12 month period.[2] The highest average financial detriment per problem was found in the insurance category, followed by home maintenance and improvements and personal banking.

5.5 The report's focus was on financial detriment, that is the financial loss associated with consumer problems. Financial loss is experienced in a number of ways, including:

(1) the cost of pursuing complaints, such as telephone calls, postage, travel costs, and obtaining expert advice and assistance;

(2) the cost of resolving the problem at the consumer's own expense, such as the cost of repairs (in 15% of cases) or purchasing replacement goods (in 13% of cases);

(3) the cost of consequential damage (an example is a washing machine leaking and causing damage to the kitchen floor);

---

[1] Office of Fair Trading, *Consumer Detriment: Assessing the frequency and impact of consumer problems with goods and services* (April 2008). Available at http://www.oft.gov.uk/shared_oft/reports/consumer_protection/oft992.pdf.

[2] Above, p 80.

(4)   the cost to the consumer, if self-employed, of lost earnings due to not being able to work while taking time to resolve the problem; and

(5)   reduction in the value of goods caused by the fault.

5.6   In financial terms, most problems were relatively small; 88% of problems were found to result in detriment less than or equal to £100. However, even small problems could cause considerable inconvenience. In around one quarter of problems, respondents spent one to four hours of their personal time rectifying the problem; in 8% of cases, consumers spent over 20 hours on the problem. Significant proportions of respondents reported feeling under stress, frustrated, angry and worried about the problem.[3] Those in lower social grades (DE) were particularly affected, experiencing greater effects both in terms of stress and their ability to spend on other items.[4]

5.7   In terms of financial detriment for faulty goods, car repairs were found to be particularly likely to cause consequential damage or inconvenience. Similarly, respondents most often had to pay to have things put right at their own expense when they experienced problems with goods such as personal computers, food and drink, and glazing products, for example, windows. The proportion of problems for which respondents had to pay for replacement was higher than average for car repairs and large domestic appliances.[5]

5.8   Looking at the length of time it takes to resolve problems, the glazing products category had a high proportion of long-term problems, 35% taking over a year to resolve.

5.9   With respect to complaining behaviour, respondents complained or did something about the problem in 64% of cases. In general, the likelihood that respondents took action increased with the price of the good or service. However, many respondents took action of some sort even where the problem related to a low value item: for goods or services priced at £30 or less, respondents took action in 58% of cases.

5.10   Even so, many respondents said that they were put off taking action because of what they described as the "hassle" involved, in terms of time and money. The most frequent way of taking action was to make a complaint to the company where the product or service was obtained. Consumers often asked the company for a replacement (21% of problems), or a refund (20%).[6] Amongst the many remedies sought and obtained by complainants, in 11% of cases a full refund was offered or obtained.

5.11   In 78% of cases, where the level of detriment was between £5 and £99, respondents indicated that the problem had had a negative effect on the likelihood of their using the company again. In 19% of cases, respondents who considered their problem resolved were still dissatisfied with the outcome.

[3]   Above, p 41.

[4]   Above, p 48.

[5]   Above, p 49.

[6]   Above, p 69.

5.12 The survey therefore showed that consumer problems are common and can cause significant distress and expense, even for apparently small items. Cars, windows and large domestic appliances are particularly likely to cause problems. Most consumers take some action (usually by complaining directly to the business), but they can easily be put off by the time and trouble it would take.

CAUSES OF ACTION: CIVIL LAW AND SOCIAL JUSTICE (2006)[7]

5.13 This report was based upon the Legal Services Research Centre surveys of justiciable problems in England and Wales. "Justiciable problems" were defined as problems which raised legal issues, even if they were not perceived as legal by those experiencing them.[8]

5.14 The survey used 18 categories of justiciable problems, including "consumer problems" arising from transactions for goods and services. Consumer problems were reported more frequently than the other 17 categories, by 10% of the population.

5.15 Those faced with consumer problems were more likely than others to take some action to resolve them, but were less likely to seek advice. Respondents either gave up trying to solve a problem or took no action at all in about 30% of consumer problems. In more than half of cases, those who had consumer problems handled the problems alone.

5.16 Respondents said they found the process of resolving consumer problems stressful, and it could even bring about ill-health.[9] Many respondents agreed to resolutions that they regarded as unfair in order to bring an end to disputes, because they found it too stressful to continue.

5.17 Socially excluded groups were found to be particularly vulnerable. Respondents receiving welfare benefits were more likely than others to report consumer problems, perhaps explained by the greater relative value to them of routine consumer transactions.

5.18 Most consumer problems related to a sum of £1,000 or less.[10] However, the report argued:

---

[7] P Pleasance with A Buck and N Balmer, *Causes of Action: Civil Law and Social Justice* (2006). It is a second edition of the report first published in 2004.

[8] For a further discussion see H Genn, *Paths to Justice: What People Do and Think About Going to Law* (1999).

[9] On 10% of occasions in the case of consumer problems, see *Causes of Action: Civil Law and Social Justice*, p 61.

[10] Above, p 137.

The fact that a justiciable problem involves a sum of £100 or less does not, of course, mean that a problem is trivial. As well as the lingering sense of injustice or betrayal of trust that can accompany justiciable problems (which can on their own introduce importance to even small value disputes), for those with little disposable income even £50 can represent a substantial loss or gain. Consistent with this, we found that the sum involved in disputes correlated with household income.[11]

5.19 The report concluded that education and enabling people to act were crucial. It explained that:

The possession of rights is meaningless if people are unaware of their existence or of the means through which they can be effected.[12]

OFT REPORT ON COMPETITION ACT AND CONSUMER RIGHTS (MAY 2006)[13]

5.20 This report detailed the main findings from two research studies on business competition and consumer rights in Britain. Here we concentrate on the findings concerning consumer rights. The first study was a consumer survey which measured the general public's knowledge of consumer rights and their confidence in using such rights. The second study was conducted amongst "consumer facing" businesses (that is those which deal directly with consumers) to measure knowledge of consumer rights legislation.

5.21 The research found that consumers generally feel protected and confident in using their rights even though they do not feel particularly well informed. The main reason for not feeling protected was not lack of laws, rather that people do not know their rights, and secondly a perception that companies try to avoid their responsibilities. Although confident to argue their case, the general public tend not to complain "unless they really have to".

5.22 The most vulnerable groups in terms of knowledge and confidence were young adults, those not working, those achieving lower levels of education and those from lower social grade groupings (many of these aspects being inter-related).[14]

---

[11] Above, p 137.

[12] Above, p 157.

[13] Competition Act & Consumer Rights, May 2006 OFT 857.

[14] Above, p 21.

5.23 When tested on various retail scenarios, the research found a mixed position in terms of knowing their rights. Most consumers knew that they were entitled to a remedy when goods are faulty (though 16% were not aware of this) and almost a third of consumers wrongly thought that they were legally entitled to a refund, repair, replacement or exchange if they simply changed their mind about a purchase.[15] Generally, consumers thought there was a time limit for returning faulty goods, the mean average being approximately three months.[16] The mean average time limit for repair or replacement was just under six months.[17]

5.24 The research showed that consumer-facing businesses also lacked knowledge of consumer rights: 48% could not mention any areas where consumer protection rules applied. A relatively high proportion of these companies had no formal procedures to help resolve customer issues: 24% had no formal consumer policies in place, generally feeling there was no need. However, 32% of companies had an "exchange/returns policy on display", which represented a substantial increase on previous years. The absence of a formal procedure was much more commonplace amongst smaller companies.[18]

5.25 When questioned on consumer rights across four different shopping scenarios, there was a widespread variation in businesses' understanding. The most conclusive viewpoint was in terms of faulty items for which the consumer had a receipt. Ninety-one percent of the business respondents were aware that consumers are legally entitled to a refund, repair or replacement for faulty goods. Forty per cent of respondents thought that consumers are legally entitled to a refund, repair or replacement if a consumer simply changes their mind.[19]

5.26 The survey showed that there was a general lack of knowledge of consumer rights among both consumers and businesses. That said, most businesses and consumers were aware of a right to return faulty goods. In fact, consumers often overestimated their right to return goods, both in terms of returning non-faulty items, and in terms of how long the right lasts.

SCOTTISH CONSUMER COUNCIL RESEARCH REPORT: KNOWLEDGE OF CONSUMER RIGHTS IN SCOTLAND (2003)[20]

5.27 The aim of this study was to find out how well informed Scottish consumers were of their rights. Previous research had suggested that Scottish consumers felt less well informed than consumers in England and Wales. The Scottish Consumer Council was, therefore, keen to explore this in greater depth. Despite contrary indications, the study found that consumers in Scotland were generally as well informed as those elsewhere in Britain. However, there were gaps in knowledge even amongst those who thought they were well informed. The report stated:

---

[15] Above, pp 6 and 47.

[16] Above, pp 6 and 49.

[17] Above, p 7.

[18] Above, pp 91 to 92.

[19] Above, pp 11 and 100.

[20] Scottish Consumer Council, *Knowledge of Consumer Rights in Scotland* (2003). Available at http://www.scotconsumer.org.uk/publications/reports/reports03/rp03know.pdf.

Confident, demanding consumers have an important role to play in making markets work effectively. But if they are to be confident and demanding, consumers must be well informed about their rights and how to go about enforcing them. They also need to know where to go for help if they have a problem with faulty goods or poor services.

5.28   Consumer problems are among the most common problems that people in Scotland are faced with on a daily basis. Almost three in ten of those who had purchased goods or services in the previous 12 months said that they had cause to complain about them.

5.29   The most common reason for complaint was defective goods or poor quality services. The category of goods and services which gave most cause for complaint was white and electrical goods, followed by communications products (including mobile phones and computers).

5.30   The vast majority (95%) of those who had cause for complaint actually complained. Of those, the majority (82%) first complained directly to the seller or service provider. Very few people sought advice about their complaint. Consumers in disadvantaged groups were significantly less likely to complain.

5.31   Many consumers did not achieve the outcome they expected. For example, in 25% of cases consumers felt they were entitled to a full refund, but only received that remedy in 7% of cases. In 40% of cases consumers believed they were entitled to a replacement (of the whole item or missing parts), but they only received that remedy in 27% of cases.

5.32   The report also showed that consumers misunderstood their legal rights. Participants were asked to answer "true" or "false" to a number of statements about their rights:

(1)   35% thought that they were entitled to a refund if they returned goods which were not faulty, but which they no longer wanted; and

(2)   67% of people believed that retailers had the right to repair faulty goods before offering a refund.

5.33   The report concluded:

It is also clear that even those who felt they were well informed were not always as knowledgeable as they believed they were. When asked about a series of specific consumer rights, many respondents gave the wrong answer.

Comparison of consumers' expectations when they complained against what actually happened provides further evidence that many people are unaware of their rights. In many instances, there was a considerable gap between what respondents thought they were entitled to, and the outcome they achieved.[21]

5.34   The report had a number of other conclusions, including:

[21]   Above, p 44.

52

(1) Consumers are generally at a disadvantage due to the imbalance of power in their relationship with a retailer. Consumer protection legislation exists to redress the balance.

(2) Whilst many consumers are confident and demanding, a significant proportion are not. Confident consumers can help drive the economy in a positive way.

(3) Consumers from disadvantaged groups often have cause to complain but do not do so, either because of a lack of knowledge about rights or a lack of advice.

(4) There is a need for improved consumer education about consumer rights and how to go about enforcing them; such education should be targeted particularly towards the disadvantaged groups of consumers identified in the research.

(5) There are indications that customer-friendly policies adopted by some high-street stores are increasing consumers' expectations beyond what they are entitled to in law. Some people assume that they are entitled to refunds when they simply change their mind about goods because many stores now offer refunds in such instances.

CONCLUSION

5.35 The key points from these four reports are:

(1) Consumer problems are common. The OFT Report on Consumer Detriment estimated that there are about 26.5 million consumer problems over a one year period, which amounted to an estimated £6.6 billion in terms of financial consumer detriment.

(2) Consumer problems can cause other problems in terms of psychological effects, such as stress and worry.

(3) Most people deal with the problem themselves, by complaining directly to the retailer, without any assistance or advice. It is therefore particularly important that consumer remedies are simple enough for consumers and consumer-facing retailers to understand.

(4) There is a widespread lack of understanding of consumer rights. For example, consumers do not know the meaning of the phrase "this shall not affect your statutory rights".

(5) Even those consumers who feel they are well informed are often not as knowledgeable as they think they are. Many overestimate their rights. Consumers' expectations are often raised by shops' returns policies and manufacturers' guarantees.

(6) On the other hand, consumers may accept what retailers tell them their policy is, even if it is less generous than the law: 16% of consumers did not know they were entitled to a legal remedy if goods were faulty.

(7)   In many cases, consumers remain dissatisfied with the outcome of disputes. Generally, this has a negative effect on the likelihood of them purchasing from that retailer again.

(8)   Poorer consumers are particularly vulnerable to the consequences of consumer problems. They are less aware of their rights, and feel the financial and non-financial effects more keenly.

PART 6
CONSUMER REMEDIES IN OTHER JURISDICTIONS

INTRODUCTION

6.1 We undertook as much comparative research as time allowed in order to find out how consumer remedies work in other jurisdictions. We are very grateful to the experts and researchers who advised us on the law in other jurisdictions, some of whom submitted papers to us.[1] We were also greatly assisted in our comparative research by the European Consumer Centres who provided input on how the law works in practice in other member states.

6.2 This Part summarises the law in the jurisdictions at which we looked. We start with three EU member states: France, Germany and Ireland. We then consider two common law jurisdictions: the USA and New Zealand. More detailed accounts of the law in those jurisdictions can be found on our website.[2]

6.3 This Part also sets out the key findings from the responses which we received to our questionnaire which was circulated to European Consumer Centres. The questionnaire itself can be found on our website.[3]

6.4 With regard to the Consumer Sales Directive (CSD), most member states found its implementation to be challenging, particularly those which already had well-developed domestic legal provisions covering the same areas as the CSD. In many states, difficulties persist today, both in interpreting the CSD and in the overlap between the CSD remedies and domestic remedies such as damages.

6.5 It seems that the "right to reject" is a concept which is familiar to many other member states as it formed part of their remedial regimes before the CSD was passed in 1999. The European Commission's green paper on guarantees for consumer goods and after-sales services[4] indicates that a "right to reject" of some description existed as a remedy for defective goods in all member states, bar one, at that time.[5] By "right to reject" we mean the consumer's right to terminate the sales contract and receive a reimbursement of the price, as a remedy of first instance, in appropriate cases.[6]

---

[1] We would extend particular thanks to Professor Simon Whittaker; Professor Hans-W Micklitz; Kai P Purnhagen; Laura Treacy; Professor John Adams and Professor Cynthia Hawes.

[2] Appendix D at www.lawcom.gov.uk and www.scotlawcom.gov.uk.

[3] Appendix C at www.lawcom.gov.uk and www.scotlawcom.gov.uk.

[4] COM(93)509 final Brussels, 15 November 1993.

[5] The member states with a "right to reject" were: Germany, Belgium, Denmark, Spain, France, Greece, Portugal, Italy, Luxembourg, the UK and Ireland. The Netherlands was the sole exception, relying primarily on the remedies of repair and replacement, with reimbursement being a secondary remedy or an option for the seller.

[6] See para 2.10.

6.6 Since the CSD, some member states have retained the "right to reject" as a separate right,[7] while others have effectively retained it by giving consumers a free choice of all four CSD remedies at first instance.[8] The "right to reject" also forms part of the remedial regimes of other jurisdictions outside of Europe, such as the USA and New Zealand.

FRANCE

6.7 In France, the requirement to implement the CSD led to a heated and lengthy debate over how it should be implemented. Should there be an amendment to the general law of sale in the Civil Code or should a supplementary set of rights for consumer buyers be inserted into the Consumer Law Code? In the end, the French government decided upon the latter option, and retained the traditional domestic remedies which had been available to consumers.

6.8 Prior to the CSD, French law governing consumers' rights in relation to faulty goods was already very complex. It provided a range of remedies under the general law of contract (based on both duties of information and contractual obligations of conformity); and also under special rules governing contracts of sale which impose a legal guarantee upon sellers in respect of latent defects. One of the arguments in favour of reform was the need to reduce this complexity.

6.9 As the legislation which implemented the CSD in France expressly retained the traditional domestic remedies, as well as being able to pursue the CSD remedies, consumers are also entitled to pursue the domestic remedies, as follows.

6.10 Purchasers of faulty goods have the right, under the **legal guarantee**, to choose whether: (a) to terminate the contract and recover their money in exchange for the goods; (b) to require a reduction in price; and/or (c) to claim damages. The first option is like the UK "right to reject".

6.11 Under the general law of contract, purchasers are entitled to damages for the non-performance of the **duties of information**, or the non-performance of the **contractual obligation of conformity.** A lack of conformity gives rise to a variety of remedies. These can include a claim for enforced proper performance, or a claim to obtain substitute performance elsewhere and damages. The purchaser may also seek retroactive termination of the contract with restitution, counter-restitution and damages. In effect this means returning the good and the purchase price, with the possibility of further damages.

6.12 The legislation which implemented the CSD also amended the legal guarantee, mentioned in paragraph 6.10 above. Traditionally, claims under the legal guarantee had to be brought within a "brief period", which was relatively short and uncertain (probably about six months). The amendment to the legal guarantee replaced "brief period" with a fixed period of two years from the discovery of the defect. In this way, the amendments extended and reinvigorated the traditional remedies which include the French "right to reject".

---

[7] This includes Ireland, France and the UK.

[8] This includes Greece, Latvia, Lithuania, Portugal and Slovenia.

GERMANY

6.13 Prior to the implementation of the CSD, German sales law was set out in the German Civil Code (the Bürgerliches Gesetzbuch or "BGB"). The BGB was passed in 1896 and commenced in 1900. As the provisions relating to sales remained largely unchanged since 1895, the law was out of date with legal practice and rather complex. To a considerable extent, legal practice had evolved to remedy problems in the market place, but legal practice did not reflect the law in the statute books.

6.14 In 1979, the German government commissioned a study on the reform of German contract law, but its proposals were never enacted. Subsequently, in 2002, the German government took the requirement to implement the CSD as an opportunity to rejuvenate the wider reforms envisaged in the project which commenced in 1979.

6.15 Therefore, in implementing the CSD, the German government undertook a major overhaul of sales law in general, and incorporated consumer law into the BGB. According to some commentators, this turned German sales law on its head, resolving some old problems, but creating some new ones.[9] The process triggered a major debate in Germany with many criticising the reforms, partly because they represented a departure from traditional German legal doctrine. In practice, the interpretation of the new regime has proved problematic for courts and academic commentators.[10]

6.16 Before the CSD was implemented, the right to specific performance only lasted until delivery of the defective goods. From the moment of delivery, the system switched to a special "warranty theory" regime, which was advantageous to the purchaser as it permitted immediate rescission of the contract. This was very similar to the UK **"right to reject"**. There was a six-month limitation period for this remedy.

6.17 Other breaches of sales contracts carried a longer limitation period. For example, there was a 30 year limitation period for misrepresentation, or if the wrong goods were delivered. The difference in limitation periods necessitated a distinction between defects in goods and breaches of ancillary duties, such as appropriate packaging, and defects in goods and consequential damage. In addition, the short limitation periods caused courts to apply tort law in certain cases since it provided a longer limitation period.

6.18 The remedies of **repair and replacement** were not available in general contract law, although they were often agreed in practice between the parties. German sales law focused on the sale of specific goods, and the remedies of rescission and price reduction. The damages regime was criticised for being too restrictive.

---

[9] P Rott, *German Sales Law Two Years After the Implementation of Directive 1999/44/EC,* German Law Journal 5, 237 to 256, 2004. For a discussion of German law in English see Zimmerman, *The New German Law of Obligations* (2005).

[10] For example, see the European Court of Justice decision *Quelle* ECJ C-404/06, in which it was held that a seller who has sold goods which are not in conformity may not require the consumer to pay compensation for the use of those goods until their replacement with new goods.

6.19   In contrast, after the 2002 reforms, the right to request cure was extended to apply *after* delivery of the goods. This switch from "warranty theory" to "performance theory" represented a major reform in German private law.

6.20   Since the 2002 reforms, the BGB contains a catalogue of remedies available to purchasers of faulty goods, the primary remedy being the purchaser's right to request cure (repair or replacement).

6.21   If this right to request cure cannot be exercised, the purchaser has the right of reduction in price or rescission of the contract. In addition, the purchaser has the right to claim damages for futile expenditure. The post-CSD damages regime in Germany goes far beyond what previously existed, including, for example, damages for delayed performance and missed performance.

6.22   The seller is automatically discharged from his duty to cure if cure is impossible, and the seller has the right to deny the purchaser's request for cure if it is disproportionately expensive. The question of what is disproportionately expensive is the subject of a large amount of debate. Despite this, no general rule has yet emerged.

6.23   In addition to general sales law remedies, consumers are often granted special protection such as the **right to withdraw from contracts**. This is granted by many retailers' standard sales terms; it allows consumers to return faulty goods and receive a refund and is similar to the UK "right to reject" and the pre-CSD German "right to reject".

IRELAND

6.24   The European Commission described Irish domestic consumer sales law as having a "pioneering, exemplary character".[11] Under the domestic regime, consumers have a primary right to reject faulty goods, and also a secondary right to request cure (repair or replacement). This has led some commentators to conclude that the Irish domestic regime provides superior protection to consumers than the CSD.[12]

6.25   In Ireland, consumer remedies for faulty goods find their basis in the Sale of Goods Act 1893, as amended by the Sale of Goods and Supply of Services Act 1980 and the European Communities (Certain Aspects of the Sale of Consumer Goods and Associated Guarantees) Regulations 2003.[13]

6.26   The Sale of Goods Act was passed in both the UK and Ireland in 1894. However, the domestic provisions in the UK and Ireland are significantly different, because in Ireland, the Sale of Goods Act was extensively amended in 1980.

---

[11]   See White, "The EC Directive on Certain Aspects of Consumer Sale and Associated Guarantees: One Step Forward, Two Steps Back?" (2000) 7(1) CLP 3.

[12]   See White, "The EC Directive on Certain Aspects of Consumer Sale and Associated Guarantees: One Step Forward, Two Steps Back?" (2000) 7(1) CLP 3; and Walley, "The Directive on Certain Aspects of the Sale of Consumer Goods and Associated Guarantees—Implications for Irish Consumer Sales Law" (2000) 18 ILT 23.

[13]   SI No 11 of 2003 implementing Directive 1999/44 EC.

6.27 Under the amendment statute,[14] the purchaser of faulty goods has the right to treat the contract as repudiated and to reject the goods (the "**right to reject**") as they would in the UK. The right to reject may be lost if the purchaser accepts the goods, in which case the remedy lies solely in damages.

6.28 Acceptance is defined in section 35 of the 1893 Act. This definition was amended in the 1980 Act[15] with the result that it varies significantly from the current UK definition of acceptance. Under the amended section 35, the buyer is deemed to have accepted the goods when:

(1) he intimates to the seller that he has accepted them; or

(2) subject to the buyer's right to examine the goods, when the goods have been delivered to the buyer and he does any act in relation to the goods which is inconsistent with the ownership of the seller; or

(3) *when without good and sufficient reason, he retains the goods without intimating to the seller that he has rejected them.*

6.29 The words "after the lapse of a reasonable time" (as found in section 35 of the 1893 Act and the UK Sale of Goods Act 1979) were substituted by the words "without good and sufficient reason" by the 1980 Act. Therefore, the issue in Ireland is not whether the buyer acted within a reasonable time, but rather whether the buyer had good and sufficient reason for not acting. It appears that this change was made to avoid the difficulties which have arisen in the UK with regard to defining "a reasonable time".[16] This wording appears to allow consumers to reject for **latent defects**.

6.30 It should also be noted that the purchaser, in addition to any right to reject goods, also has the right to sue for **damages** for breach of contract. The purchaser can either maintain an action for damages against the seller or set off the breach against the purchase price of the goods.[17]

6.31 Even before the CSD, the Irish legislation provided that where the consumer had accepted the goods, the consumer was entitled to request that the seller **cure** the fault (by repair or replacement). If the seller refused to do so or failed to do so within a reasonable period, the consumer had the choice either to reject the faulty goods or have the defect remedied elsewhere and claim for the cost against the seller.[18] Therefore, the **right to reject could be revived**.

---

14   Sale of Goods Act 1893, s 11(2) as amended by s 10 of the Sale of Goods and Supply of Services Act 1980.

15   By s 20 of the Sale of Goods and Supply of Services Act 1980.

16   It is reported that the amendment was made to reverse the decision in *Lee v York Coach and Marine Ltd* [1977] RTR 35. In that case the buyer of a defective car did not reject the goods outright but rather spent six months attempting to have it repaired and to have the garage remedy the problem. The buyer was deemed to have accepted the goods. See Grogan, King and Donelan, *Sale of Goods and Supply of Services, A Guide to the Legislation* (1982), p 39.

17   Sale of Goods Act 1893, s 53 as amended by s 21 of the Sale of Goods and Supply of Services Act 1980.

18   As above.

6.32   The right to reject is the primary right given to consumers by traditional domestic legislation. The right to cure is secondary and "operates to provide a consumer buyer with a second chance to reject".[19]

6.33   The **CSD** was implemented into Irish law by way of statutory instrument. In 2003 the text of the CSD was transposed into the Consumer Sales Regulations.[20] The implementation did not involve any alteration to the existing remedies under domestic legislation. The Regulations explicitly state that they are in addition to and not in substitution of the Sale of Goods Acts.

6.34   Therefore, the transposition of the CSD has led to an anomaly in Irish consumer sales law. Under the Sale of Goods Acts 1893 and 1980, the consumer's primary means of redress is the right to reject the faulty goods. By contrast, under the Consumer Sales Regulations 2003, the repair or replacement of the defective goods is the initial remedy. It has been noted that this shifts the balance in favour of the seller when compared to the traditional domestic position.[21]

6.35   In addition, under section 8 of the Consumer Sales Regulations, the consumer does not have a right to rescind the contract if the lack of conformity is minor. However, under domestic law, the consumer has the right to repudiate the contract if a condition has been breached. This right does not depend on the severity of the breach.

THE UNITED STATES OF AMERICA

6.36   In the USA, sales law is legislated at state level. There is no single sales law that applies across the 50 states. Despite this, there is a great deal of uniformity. It has been achieved by individual states enacting legislation based upon "uniform" sales laws, which were drawn up by legal scholars at a national level. The first of these was the Uniform Sales Act 1906, which was similar to the Sale of Goods Act 1893 in the UK. At its peak, this law was adopted by over 80% of the states.[22]

6.37   The Uniform Sales Act was replaced by the Uniform Commercial Code (UCC), which, by 1967, had been adopted by all states except Louisiana. Nevertheless, state legislation does not always follow the UCC in all respects.

6.38   The UCC provides a **right to reject** which is drafted in similar terms to the right to reject under the Sale of Goods Act 1979 in the UK. Purchasers of faulty goods may exercise their right to reject provided that the goods have not been accepted, and that the right to reject is exercised within a reasonable time.

---

[19]   White, "The EC Directive on Certain Aspects of Consumer Sale and Associated Guarantees: One Step Forward, Two Steps Back?" (2000) 7(1) CLP 3 at 10.

[20]   EC (Certain Aspects of the Sale of Consumer Goods and Associated Guarantees) Regulations 2003.

[21]   White, "The EC Directive on Certain Aspects of Consumer Sale and Associated Guarantees: One Step Forward, Two Steps Back?" (2000) 7(1) CLP 3 at 10.
Walley notes, "the complex hierarchy of remedies is not as potent as the immediate right to reject goods for breach of an implied condition under Irish law" in "The Directive on Certain Aspects of the Sale of Consumer Goods and Associated Guarantees—Implications for Irish Consumer Sales Law" (2000) 18 ILT 23 at 23.

[22]   *Corbin on Contracts* (1993), § 1.21.

6.39   Goods are accepted when the purchaser fails to make an effective rejection despite having had a reasonable opportunity to inspect the goods. Goods are also accepted upon express notification of acceptance by the purchaser, or where the purchaser (subject to having had a reasonable opportunity to inspect) has used the goods in a way that is inconsistent with the seller's ownership of them. The length of the "reasonable time" for rejection appears to depend on the facts of the case, including the seller's behaviour. It has been described as "a persistently litigated yet perpetually confused question".[23]

6.40   In addition to the rules on acceptance, there are also rather complex rules on the purchaser's **right to revoke acceptance**, which can permit purchasers to return goods long after purchase. There are also rules on the seller's **right to cure,** which permit the seller to satisfy the contract by making a conforming delivery if the time for performance has not yet expired and, in some limited circumstances, after the time for performance has expired. An extended period exists in which the purchaser can revoke acceptance with respect to **latent defects**, and the seller has no right to cure in these cases.

6.41   Apart from the UCC, there is also the **Magnuson-Moss Act 1975**. This Act applies across the USA and stipulates rules which apply when goods are sold with a written warranty. The Act aims to encourage the provision of better information from suppliers of warranties. "Full warranties" must comply with certain minimum standards. Whilst there is no such guaranteed minimum level of protection where goods are sold with "limited warranties", there is a requirement that the warranty should fully and conspicuously disclose its terms and conditions in simple language.

6.42   In addition, every state in the USA has a **lemon law** to protect purchasers of new cars which are deemed to be irredeemably faulty.[24] Whilst these laws differ from state to state, there are some common elements evident in the majority of the states. Generally, lemon laws cover faults which significantly impair the use, market value or safety of the vehicle. Where there is a qualifying fault, they require the manufacturer to remedy the fault. After a reasonable number of attempts at repair, or if repairs are not undertaken within a reasonable time, secondary remedies are triggered, such as replacement or a refund of the price.

NEW ZEALAND

6.43   The Consumer Guarantees Act 1993 introduced a new regime of consumer rights and remedies with the aim of ensuring that consumers enjoyed greater protection than was previously available.

6.44   It created several statutory guarantees, and provided rights of redress against suppliers and manufacturers. With regard to the supply of goods to consumers, the guarantees include guarantees as to title, quality, fitness for purpose and compliance with description and sample.

---

[23]   J J White and R S Summers, *Uniform Commercial Code* (2000) p 318.

[24]   The primary focus of many states' lemon laws is new cars, however, some lemon laws provide protection for used car purchases.

6.45   The Consumer Guarantees Act provides that where goods are supplied to a consumer there is a guarantee that the goods are of acceptable quality. Where the failure in the goods cannot be remedied or is of a "substantial character", the **consumer may reject the goods**, or obtain compensation from the supplier for any reduction in the value of the goods below their purchase price.

6.46   Failure is of a "substantial character" in the following circumstances: the goods would not have been acquired by a reasonable consumer fully acquainted with the nature and extent of the failure; the goods depart in one or more significant respects from their description or any sample; the goods are substantially unfit for a purpose for which goods of the type in question are commonly supplied or a particular purpose made known to the supplier or represented by the supplier to be a purpose for which the goods would be fit; or the goods are not of acceptable quality because they are unsafe.

6.47   The right to reject goods is lost if, for example, the right is not exercised within a reasonable time, or if the consumer has disposed of the goods. What constitutes a reasonable time for rejection depends upon the period in which it would be reasonable to expect the defect to become apparent, having regard to the type of goods, the use to which a consumer is likely to put them, the length of time for which it is reasonable to use them and the amount of use which is reasonable before the defect becomes apparent.[25]

6.48   Where the failure to comply with the guarantee can be remedied, the **consumer may require the supplier to remedy the failure** within a reasonable time. This means repairing the goods or curing the defect, or replacing the goods. If the supplier does not do so, or does not do so within a reasonable time, the consumer may have the failure remedied elsewhere and obtain all reasonable costs from the supplier, or may reject the goods.

THE EUROPEAN CONSUMER CENTRE QUESTIONNAIRE

Introduction

6.49   We were particularly interested to find out about the consumer experience in the rest of Europe. We wanted to know how the CSD operates in practice and which other remedies are offered. We devised a questionnaire (available on our website), focussing on some of the areas of the CSD which stakeholders say cause difficulties. We are grateful to the UK European Consumer Centre which circulated our questionnaire to the other 26 European Consumer Centres, and returned the responses to us. We received 17 responses.

6.50   We found that consumers returning goods are not necessarily dealt with according to the strict letter of the law. Some are dealt with according to shop policies which vary widely and are not limited to repair or replacement. The responses indicate that many retailers across Europe offer better remedies than those required by the CSD in order to compete in the market place and attract custom. It appears that retailers recognise that consumers may not be satisfied with repair or replacement as their only remedies of first instance.

---

[25] Consumer Guarantees Act 1993, s 20(2).

6.51 There are a wide variety of policies and remedies across Europe, very much depending on the retailer and the market place within which it operates. Remedies which are offered at first instance include: refunds (even for minor or cosmetic defects); no-quibble money-back guarantees within a set time limit (for example, 24 hours or one month); exchanges for other products (the consumer paying the difference in price if necessary); vouchers; discounts and credit notes.

6.52 This is similar to the UK consumer experience, although there is some indication that voluntary returns policies in the UK may have fewer variations than in the rest of Europe, and possibly be more prevalent.

6.53 The other major finding is that there is apparently a wide variation in approaches across Europe with respect to the problematic areas of the CSD. The main problematic areas can be summarised by the following questions: How many repairs should a consumer be expected to accept? What is a reasonable time for repairs? What is "significant inconvenience"?

6.54 A further finding is that the vast majority of respondents appear to have a legal mechanism of some description for consumers to claim compensation (damages) for consequential loss.

"Significant inconvenience" and "reasonable time"

6.55 The maximum number of repairs which the consumer can reasonably be expected to accept before demanding another remedy varies widely in the responses, ranging from one attempt per item to three attempts per fault. The former means that the retailer is only allowed one attempt at repair per item regardless of the number of faults; the latter means that if there are numerous faults occurring in one item, the retailer is permitted to repair each fault three times. Some respondents said that if numerous faults occurred at the same time, or if a fault is sufficiently serious, the consumer might have the right to withdraw from the contract and get a refund, or demand a replacement.

6.56 On the question of how long repairs should reasonably take, some respondents said that there are no legal rules in their jurisdiction at all and it just depends on the facts of the case. Other respondents were able to offer guidelines, once again across a wide spectrum from eight days to one month. Some respondents indicated that if an item had been purchased for a special occasion the period should be shorter. One respondent said that if a defect cannot be repaired within 30 days the consumer can withdraw from the contract and get a refund. Two respondents said that if repairs take longer than a week the retailer would have to lend the consumer a similar item for use whilst repairs were taking place. With respect to the dangerous car scenario,[26] several respondents said that a consumer can demand a refund if there is a significant lack of conformity or a serious defect.

---

[26] See Appendix C, Scenario 2 (at www.lawcom.gov.uk and www.scotlawcom.gov.uk).

Other issues

6.57   When asked about the number of replacements a consumer can reasonably be expected to accept, the most common answer was "one". Some respondents explicitly said that, if that replacement failed, the consumer would be entitled to a refund and would not have to accept an alternative remedy.

6.58   The majority of respondents said that while the choice between repair or replacement is legally the consumer's, in practice it is the retailer who chooses.

PART 7
THE CASE FOR REFORM

INTRODUCTION

7.1 In Parts 2 and 3 of this Consultation Paper we set out our understanding of the current law. In this Part, we discuss the problem areas in more detail, and show that many of the difficulties are not only theoretical, but also represent problems in practice.

7.2 In summary, the criticisms of the current regime fall into three broad categories:

(1) Problems with the traditional domestic remedies. In particular, there is uncertainty as what constitutes a reasonable time in the context of the "right to reject". Furthermore the available remedies may vary according to the type of supply contract.

(2) The uneasy co-existence of two regimes under the Sale of Goods Act 1979 (SoGA), that is the European remedies (from the Consumer Sales Directive) and traditional UK remedies. This leads to complex law. Examples include the different burdens of proof which apply, and the possible confusion between the right to reject and rescission.

(3) Problems with the Consumer Sales Directive (CSD) itself. This includes the meaning of terms such as "significant inconvenience", "reasonable time", "impossible" and "disproportionate"; the possibility of reducing the amount of a refund after rescission to allow for use; and the fact that the CSD does not apply to all supply of goods contracts.

THE DAVIDSON REVIEW

7.3 As discussed in Part 1, this project was recommended by the Davidson Review, set up in 2005 to look at how the UK implemented European legislation. The CSD was cited as an example of "double-banking", where the UK had failed to streamline the overlap between existing law and the new EU-sourced legislation.

7.4 The Review noted criticism from commentators, business and consumer groups that, following the implementation of the CSD, the remedies available to consumers had become too complicated. It was not easy for consumers to understand what their rights were and this led to disputes. For example, Consumer Direct said that the fact that there were two different remedy routes which used different language, different concepts and different burdens of proof added difficulty and uncertainty in providing advice. The Report concluded:

> Making the law on consumer remedies in sale of goods and similar contracts more coherent will benefit both consumers and business. If consumers have a better understanding of their statutory rights if they buy goods, they will have more confidence in using their rights and be able to enforce them more easily. Business can also benefit through improved relations with customers.[1]

7.5 The Review noted that the impact of implementing the CSD is significant, in that the law in the UK governing consumer sales is relied on every day in relation to a large number of transactions. The CSD covers all consumer purchases of goods, which the Review estimated to be worth around £250 billion a year.[2]

STAKEHOLDER FEEDBACK

7.6 At the beginning of this project, we met a wide range of stakeholders, including retailers, consumer groups and academics.[3] We were particularly interested in the areas which proved to be problematic in practice, and how the law could be simplified. As we said in 2004:[4]

> Consumer law affects everyone in their day-to-day dealings. We agree with the [Department of Trade and Industry] that it is therefore particularly important that it should be accessible and comprehensible – if not to individual consumers, at least to advisers without legal training. Businesses also need to find out about the law and understand it without expensive legal advice.

7.7 The feedback from our discussions with retailers and consumer groups alike was that the main need now was to clarify and simplify the law rather than to effect radical reform. Since providing feedback to the Davidson Review, stakeholders have become more familiar with the new provisions. They thought that the law in this area largely works, or as one retailer said: "the law has been made to work", although various ambiguities need to be elucidated and simplified.

7.8 Generally, retailers accepted that the existing level of consumer protection should be maintained. Among consumer groups there was strong support for retaining the traditional domestic remedies – the right to reject and damages. These remedies are generally considered to be fundamental elements of the UK system. The right to reject was thought to be fair and easy to understand in principle. This feedback is supported by the FDS research which found that consumers felt strongly that they did not want to lose the right to reject.[5]

---

[1] Davidson Review, *Final Report* (November 2006) para 3.23.

[2] Above, para 3.10. Spending on consumer goods has since increased to approximately £400 billion in 2007, Office for National Statistics, *Consumer Trends: Quarter 4 2007* (2008).

[3] See Appendix B for a list of the people and organisations we met from January to April 2008.

[4] Law Commission, *Simplifying Consumer Legislation: A response from the Law Commission to the DTI's Consultative Document on Strategy* (2004).

[5] FDS Report, see Appendix A.

7.9   We asked how the law could be made to work better. Stakeholders who dealt daily with disputes about faulty goods highlighted grey areas in the law, which would benefit from simplification and guidance. These included:

    (1)   The length of a reasonable time in the context of the right to reject;

    (2)   How the different regimes (traditional UK remedies and the CSD remedies) work together and how to move between the different regimes;

    (3)   How to progress between CSD tiers; and

    (4)   The meaning of certain CSD terms.

7.10   Such clarification was thought to be more beneficial than major change. Both retailers and consumer advisors thought that major legal change would have cost implications, especially in retraining staff and changing procedures. They felt that this would not be justified.

7.11   As discussed in Parts 4 and 5, consumers are not clear about their legal rights. There is a troubling and almost universal confusion amongst consumers about the phrase "This shall not affect your statutory rights", found at the bottom of retailers' returns policies. This phrase can have the effect of misleading consumers about their rights, in some circumstances causing consumers to think that they have fewer rights than they actually have.

7.12   Consumer groups take the view that the effect of this type of uncertainty is to shift the bargaining power in favour of the retailer. Consumers are hesitant to assert their legal rights when they do not know what those rights are. On the other hand, retailers point out that consumers' lack of knowledge of their legal rights can lead them to over-estimate their rights, which puts retailers at a disadvantage and causes unnecessary disputes.

EXPLORING THE COMPLEXITIES OF THE LAW

The example of a faulty washing machine

7.13   Many of the problems which stakeholders have told us about present difficulties in practice. In the discussion that follows, we use the following typical faulty washing machine scenario to illustrate some of the practical problems and complexities that the current law presents for consumers and retailers:

> A consumer (C) buys a washing machine. C uses it once and goes on holiday for three weeks. On C's return (four weeks after purchase), C uses the machine for a week before it breaks down. C contacts the retailer. The retailer promises to arrange a repair. The retailer rings back several days later and informs C that a repairman will come to fix the machine. The repairman comes out and repairs the fault, but only a few days later the machine breaks again, for a different reason (Fault (2)). C complains to the retailer and a week later (7 weeks after purchase), C purports to reject the machine.

7.14   What are C's legal rights? Can C reject the machine? When will C lose the right to reject because C is deemed to have accepted it? When does time begin to run? Which other remedies are available? And finally, would the answer be different if C had bought the washing machine on hire purchase or as part of a fitted kitchen?

7.15   This scenario is typical of the type of query that consumers put to consumer advisers every day. In an ideal world, a consumer adviser should be able to provide a clear, simple answer and that is what consumers seek. Unfortunately, the law in this area is complex, uncertain and unsuitable for any consumer wanting a quick reply to their query. This simple scenario raises various nuances of the law which are unlikely to be appreciated by the average person. In the discussion that follows we use this example to illustrate how the various complexities of the law impact on typical problems that people encounter on a day to day basis.

Different burdens of proof

7.16   Looking at the faulty washing machine scenario, the first thing C must show is that there has been a breach of contract, in particular of the term implied by section 14 of SoGA (about quality and fitness). How C does this will depend on which remedy C wants to pursue.

7.17   If C wishes to rely on a CSD remedy (that is, repair, replacement, rescission or reduction in price), C can rely on section 48A of SoGA. This section lays down a presumption that where the goods do not conform to the contract at any time within the first six months, they are presumed not to have conformed at the time of sale.

7.18   If, on the other hand, C wishes to reject under SoGA, or to claim damages, C cannot rely on the presumption. C will have to show that the defect existed at the time of the sale, and did not arise later. This illustrates that the burden of proof to show that goods are faulty varies depending on which set of remedies are pursued.

7.19   It is unlikely that consumers would appreciate that within the first six months there is a different burden of proof when attempting to show the goods are not of satisfactory quality, depending on whether they claim to reject or rescind.

The right to reject – what is a reasonable time?

7.20   In order to reject the goods, C must show that the right to reject has not been lost by acceptance. In particular, C has to show that they have not retained the goods beyond a reasonable time.

7.21 In the example, C rejects the washing machine seven weeks after purchase. Is seven weeks a reasonable time to test a washing machine? In *Bernstein*[6] a car was held to be accepted after only three weeks, which would suggest that seven weeks is too long. However, it appears that in calculating what amounts to "a reasonable time" certain periods may be discounted. In *Bernstein* the period of illness was discounted, so it may be possible to argue that the holiday period should also be discounted, which would reduce the period to four weeks.

7.22 Does the week long period between the request for repair and repair being effected count towards a reasonable time? As we have seen,[7] the cases (*Clegg*[8] and *Jones*[9]) are inconsistent. The effect of the 2002 Regulations seems to be that the period will not be counted.[10] This would reduce the period to three weeks.

7.23 Is three weeks beyond a reasonable time? Given the result in *Bernstein* it might seem so, but after the 1994 amendments to SoGA, it is questionable whether *Bernstein* is good law. Ultimately it is a question of fact. One factor which might be important is whether the fault arose from a particular wash cycle that was not used immediately. The complexities involved in assessing a reasonable time are discussed more fully in Part 3 of this Consultation Paper.

7.24 The question of how long "a reasonable time" is before goods are held to be accepted is particularly problematic in cases where there is a considerable delay before the goods are inspected, or there are delays while negotiations or repairs are undertaken.

Practical problems for a consumer asserting the right to reject

7.25 The legal uncertainty may cause practical problems for a consumer attempting to reject goods. If a consumer asserts the right to reject in the face of opposition from the retailer, the consumer will not receive their money back but, at the same time, will not be able to use the goods. The problem is compounded if the item is large and the retailer will not accept the return of the item. This means that, for example, a washing machine is left in the consumer's kitchen or a car is left on the consumer's driveway, in either case causing an obstruction.

---

[6] *Bernstein v Pamson Motors (Golders Green) Limited* [1987] 2 All ER 220.

[7] See paras 3.33 to 3.37 and 3.44 to 3.46.

[8] *Clegg v Andersson T/A Nordic Marine* [2003] EWCA Civ 320; [2003] 1 All ER (Comm) 721.

[9] *Jones v Gallagher (trading as Gallery Kitchens and Bathrooms)* [2004] EWCA Civ 10; [2005] 1 Lloyd's Reports 377.

[10] The Sale and Supply of Goods to Consumers Regulations 2002 may impliedly provide the answer. SoGA, s 48D provides that if a request for repair or replacement has been made, the buyer cannot reject the goods until the seller has been given a reasonable time to repair or replace. The effect of this must be that time does not run for the purposes of acceptance while repair is being requested. Otherwise, the right to reject could be lost during a period where the buyer was not entitled to exercise it.

7.26 If the retailer is intransigent, litigation may be the only way a consumer can obtain the return of the money they have paid to the retailer. Without a refund, a consumer may not be in a financial position to buy a replacement item. This is a particular problem if the item is expensive, and/or an essential item which the consumer cannot manage without for any significant length of time. In these cases, fearing a lengthy dispute and the uncertainties of litigation, a consumer is likely, albeit reluctantly, to accept a repair if that is the only way to gain the co-operation of the retailer. As Bridge has commented:

> A buyer, particularly one who is a consumer, requires a degree of nerve to exercise rejection rights. First of all, the uncertainty of the rejection period makes it difficult to give advice on the subject. Further, if the buyer has paid for the goods, they will have to be put out of commission if the rejection is to pass the test of unequivocality. Although rejected goods need not be returned to the seller, the buyer of a defective car, for example, is likely to wait a long time for the seller to come and collect it and may not have the resources to provide for alternative transport in the meantime. All the while, the car will be depreciating and suffering from neglect. Returning the car and keys to the seller may prove to be tactically more effective. If payment is outstanding, the buyer faces a problem common to all contracting parties exercising uncertain termination rights. If the buyer has inadvertently accepted the goods, a repudiation of the contract will turn out to be unlawful and the buyer will be open to an action by the seller.[11]

The right to reject - latent defects and unexamined goods

7.27 Some commentators and consumer advisers have raised further difficulties with regard to the right to reject. What is the status of defects which do not come to light for some time? It has been argued that the right to reject should cover latent defects. One method of doing this would be to dispense with the rules on acceptance, and apply the rules on affirmation (or, in Scotland, personal bar/waiver) to all sale and supply of goods contracts. This would mean that a consumer would be able to reject goods unless they had affirmed the contract or were personally barred from rejecting them following the discovery of the fault.

7.28 Macleod gives an example, derived from the Law Commissions' 1987 report, of a washing machine with various cycles. He argues that even if it takes weeks for a consumer to test out all the various cycles on the machine, the consumer should still be able to reject if the last one proves defective.[12] However, what if a consumer never tests one of the cycles during the first year because there has been no cause to use it? Should there be a right to reject even after that time?

---

[11] M G Bridge, *The Sale of Goods* (1997) p 176.

[12] J K Macleod, *Consumer Sales Law* (2002) para 29.07.

7.29 What about the related subject of goods which are not opened? Macleod suggests the example of skis bought at an end of ski-season sale. Many Christmas gifts may be bought some time in advance. Does time run in these circumstances? This scenario was raised in the Standing Committee debate; it was considered that if the skis were purchased and left unused in a cupboard for one or even two years, a reasonable court would discount that period so that the reasonable period would be extended.[13]

7.30 Conversely, we know from our discussions that in the interests of certainty retailers are generally keen for the length of time for rejection to be kept quite short. They feel strongly that it should not be extended. It is also thought that extending the time for rejection might encourage abuse by some consumers who may use an item for a period of time, and then seek a refund when they no longer need it. In practice, many retailers make some allowance for Christmas gifts, using judgment and discretion in these cases to allow refunds after longer periods than usual. Alternatively, they offer "gift receipts" which make special provision for the return of gifts.

Rejection versus rescission

7.31 Referring back to our faulty washing machine scenario, if C is not entitled to *reject*, C may be able to *rescind*. This is one of the CSD remedies, so the presumption in section 48A of SoGA discussed in paragraph 2.38 above will apply. However, before a consumer can purport to rescind, they must show that they are entitled to invoke this second tier remedy.[14]

7.32 This means that C can rescind if they have made a request for repair which has not been complied with within "a reasonable time" or without causing them "significant inconvenience". There is some residual doubt as to whether a repair requested for a different reason (as in the present case) is sufficient.[15] It may be found that C has to request repair of the specific fault first (Fault (2)), before invoking the second tier remedies.

7.33 Furthermore, if C makes a further request for repair, C will not be entitled to reject under SoGA until a reasonable time for repair has expired. This leads to further questions about what amounts to "a reasonable time" and "significant inconvenience".[16]

7.34 The average consumer is unlikely to appreciate the difference between the short-term right to *reject* and the longer-term right to *rescind*, which can only be exercised after the exhaustion of the first tier remedies.

---

[13] House of Commons Standing Committee C, 16 March 1994, col 37.

[14] For a discussion of the two tier approach, see paras 2.30 to 2.37.

[15] See below, paras 7.54 to 7.56.

[16] See below, paras 7.53 to 7.59.

7.35 Hogg wrote that this "new double right to rescind" is confusing for consumers. If a retailer tells consumers that they cannot exercise their right to rescind until they have first requested repair or replacement, possibly even citing SoGA to this effect, consumers are highly unlikely to realise that this requirement does not affect their short-term right to reject.[17]

Rescission – reduction for use of goods

7.36 In the faulty washing machine scenario in paragraph 7.13, if C rescinds, the retailer may be entitled to make a deduction from the purchase price, so C will receive a refund less the deduction for use that they have had during the seven weeks. How this is assessed is unclear. Is it based on second hand value of the machine, the cost of hire, or the machine's purchase price spread over the whole of its expected life? And how should the fact the machine did not function properly for at least two of the weeks be factored in?

7.37 BERR's *Trader's Guide* begins by suggesting that the purchase price should be spread over the expected life of the product. Thus if a spin dryer costing £99 was two thirds of the way through its expected life when the fault developed, the consumer's use would be valued at £66 (and only £33 returned). However, the guide goes on to state that "account might also need to be taken of the fact that goods tend to depreciate more quickly in the early years of their life span". This would suggest that one might look at the second hand value of the goods.[18]

7.38 Willett and others are critical of the use of the second-hand value as a means of assessing the extent of any partial refund. They argue that the correct measure should be based on how long the goods should have lasted – if, for example, the washing machine had an expected life-span of five years, then if it breaks down after a year, the deduction should typically be 20% of the price.[19] In support of this view, it can be said that the rapid depreciation which tends to occur early in the life of a product is essentially a reflection of the fact that the product has become second-hand. The consumer expects the product to last for a normal life-span, however, and thus the benefit which he or she receives from its use is more properly assessed on the basis of straight-line depreciation (as usually occurs in accounting practice).

---

[17] M Hogg, "The consumer's right to rescind under the Sale of Goods Act: A tale of two remedies" 2003 SLT (News) 277.

[18] Department of Trade and Industry, *A Trader's Guide: The Law Relating to the Supply of Goods and Services* (2005) p 13.

[19] C Willett, M Morgan-Taylor and A Naidoo, "The Sale and Supply of Goods to Consumers Regulations" [2004] *Journal of Business Law* 94 at 114 to 115.

7.39　In practice, however, the calculation will be more complex than this. In order to reach a second tier remedy the trader will typically have made several attempts at repair, leading to unreasonable delay and/or significant inconvenience. It is unclear whether C can try to set-off any damages for the significant inconvenience they have experienced against the deduction for use. The new remedies do not affect the right to sue for damages. It would seem unfair that the consumer's refund should be reduced to take account of the use of the (defective) goods if the consumer cannot set off these damages against the allowance for use. In theory, the consumer could sue for damages, but consumers seldom bring such claims to court and arguably a consumer remedy regime should provide a practical alternative to litigation.

Damages more generally

7.40　The question about whether a consumer can set off damages against an allowance for use following rescission leads to a more general discussion about the damages payable in a typical consumer case, where other financial loss has flowed from the purchase of faulty goods. Stakeholder feedback indicates that, in practice, consumers do not routinely obtain this type of financial compensation even where they have suffered relevant financial loss. Consumer groups have told us that consumers often ask about whether they can claim damages for financial loss, and for inconvenience. It has been suggested that the law would benefit from clarification.[20]

7.41　A claimant can usually claim for losses which are within the contracting parties' "reasonable contemplation as a not unlikely result" of the breach of contract.[21] In commercial cases, where goods are essential for business, the loss of normal business profits can be claimed.[22]

7.42　In the faulty washing machine scenario, the lack of a washing machine has not prevented C from working, but arranging for the repair may have done so. This does seem to be a likely result of the original breakdown of the machine. There may be an argument for the payment of the consumer's lost earnings, if any; and also for the cost of the use of a laundrette whilst the machine is out of use.

7.43　If the washing machine is repaired, so that the defect in the product has been corrected, the contract is thereby fulfilled. However, C is not just entitled to goods that comply with the contract, but is also entitled to be placed in the position in which they would have been had the goods been in conformity in the first place.

---

[20]　The relevant common law principles are set out in *Hadley v Baxendale* (1854) 9 Exch 341; *Victoria Laundry (Windsor) Ltd v Newman Industries Ltd* [1949] 2 KB 528; and *The Heron II* [1969] 1 AC 350.

[21]　*Chitty on Contracts* (29th ed 2004) para 26-047. See also the discussion in W W McBryde, *The Law of Contract in Scotland* (3rd ed 2007) paras 22.65 to 22.69.

[22]　*Hadley v Baxendale* (1854) 9 Exch 341.

7.44 Moving on to a connected issue, the FDS research shows that in some cases consumers may feel that they should be compensated for distress and inconvenience caused by faulty goods and/or the repair and replacement process. Generally speaking, damages are not recoverable under these heads in English law. However, where part of the object of a contract is to provide pleasure, relaxation or peace of mind, damages for disappointment can be awarded.[23]

7.45 In Scots law, damages are available for trouble and inconvenience resulting from a breach of contract.[24] Scots law differentiates between damages for "trouble and inconvenience", and damages for "mental distress" or "hurt feelings" (solatium).[25] Solatium can provide the basis of a claim where, because of the nature of the contract, "the likelihood of distress was or ought to have been in the contemplation of the defender at the time of the contract".[26]

Other supply contracts

7.46 As discussed in Part 2, the analysis of the faulty washing machine scenario would be different if the transaction were effected by a non-sales contract, such as hire purchase, exchange or a contract for work and materials. This distinction may not be apparent to a consumer, but is nevertheless important.

7.47 Instead of looking at whether the consumer had accepted the goods, in England and Wales the court would need to consider whether the consumer had affirmed the contract and, in Scotland, whether the consumer was personally barred through waiver from insisting on the return of the goods.[27] This gives the consumer far longer to reject faulty goods.

7.48 If the washing machine in our scenario were bought as part of a fitted kitchen, the initial question is whether the supply of the washing machine forms part of a work and materials contract, or is a severable contract for sale. If the former, then the consumer will almost certainly be entitled to reject the machine, as they have done nothing to affirm the contract or to waive their rights under the contract. Unlike hire purchase, the CSD remedies are available, so the consumer also has the right to ask for repair or replacement.

---

[23] *Farley v Skinner* [2001] UKHL 49; [2002] 2 AC 732.

[24] *Webster & Co v Cramond Iron Co* (1875) 2R 752; *Wilkie v Brown* 2003 SC 573.

[25] MacQueen and Thomson, *Contract Law in Scotland* (2nd ed 2007) para 6.28.

[26] Discussion Paper on Remedies for Breach of Contract (1999) Scot Law Com No 109 para 8.24; *Diesen v Samson* 1971 SLT (Sh Ct) 49; *Colston v Marshall* 1993 SLT (Sh Ct) 40.

[27] Except conditional sales, where the position is the same as for a simple sale.

7.49   If the washing machine were bought on hire purchase, then the question is also one of affirmation or waiver rather than acceptance, giving the consumer a right to reject the machine after the seven weeks. There may be some argument about whether the consumer is entitled to a full refund or must give some allowance for use. Given that the machine was only functional for a few days, and the consumer has experienced some inconvenience, it is likely that a court would allow a full refund.[28] The consumer does not have right to a repair or replacement, and would have to negotiate these with the supplier.

Problems with the CSD remedies in more detail

Two tiers

7.50   As explained in Part 2, the CSD sets out four possible remedies: repair; replacement; rescission; and reduction in price. The consumer does not have a free choice among them. Instead there is a two tier approach.

7.51   The first tier remedies are replacement and repair. The consumer can request replacement[29] or repair under section 48A of SoGA and the seller is required to comply with this within a "reasonable time" and without causing "significant inconvenience" to the buyer.[30] The seller is not obliged to comply with this request where the remedy is "impossible", or where it is "disproportionate"[31] in comparison to the other three remedies.

7.52   The second tier of remedies comes into play if the first tier is impossible or disproportionate, or if the seller does not (or cannot) comply with the request for replacement or repair within a reasonable time. In these circumstances, the consumer can ask for a reduction in price, or rescission of the contract.[32] Although this seems relatively straightforward, much remains unclear. There is confusion about how to move between the tiers, and who chooses the remedy, and also the terms which are used.

---

[28] See the discussion on this point at paras 2.53 to 2.56.

[29] It is not entirely clear whether the seller can replace the goods with a second-hand product of equivalent age – ie if the machine breaks down after six months, can the retailer supply a six-month old washing machine? There is anecdotal evidence to suggest that this may occur in practice. While it seems likely that the directive envisaged a new replacement, there is still residual doubt.

[30] SoGA s 48B(5) provides
        Any question as to what is a reasonable time or significant inconvenience is to
        be determined by reference to – (a) the nature of the goods and (b) the purpose
        for which the goods were acquired.

[31] Above, s 48B(4) provides
        One remedy is disproportionate in comparison to the other if the one imposes
        costs on the seller which, in comparison to those imposed by the other, are
        unreasonable, taking into account – (a) the value which the goods would have if
        they conformed to the contract of sale, (b) the significance of the lack of
        conformity, and (c) whether the other remedy could be effected without
        significant inconvenience to the buyer.

[32] Above, s 48C.

Terms

7.53   The feedback we have received from stakeholders indicates that some of the terminology in the CSD provisions is problematic, so that there are difficulties in applying the CSD remedies in practice. For example, what is the meaning of "significant inconvenience" and "reasonable time"?

7.54   In our faulty washing machine scenario, the consumer has already allowed one attempt at repair. How many attempts at repair must C accept before passing the threshold of "significant inconvenience", so as to be allowed to move on to the second tier remedies? In terms of the time C will have to wait for a repair, how long is unreasonable? Should more attempts at repair be permitted if there is more than one fault? How subjective is the test? The failure of the washing machine may be a significant inconvenience to a large family but only a minor inconvenience to someone living alone.

7.55   The CSD provides that the judgment about whether the seller has failed to carry out a repair, or provide a replacement, "within a reasonable time and without significant inconvenience" should take into account "the nature of the goods and the purpose for which the consumer required the goods".[33]

7.56   The reasonableness of the time and the significance of the inconvenience are questions of fact, and there is no way that this could ever be defined comprehensively. But the degree of uncertainty and lack of guidelines leads to confusion and disputes in practice. As we discussed in Part 6, our survey of European Consumer Centres across Europe found a substantial variation in approach. For example, some centres thought one repair per item was enough, while others would accept up to three repairs per fault.

7.57   With regard to the number of repairs which should be permitted where there is a series of faults, section 61 of SoGA defines repair thus:

> "repair" means in cases where there is a lack of conformity in goods for the purposes of section 48F of this Act, to bring the goods into conformity with the contract.

7.58   Applying this definition of "repair" to our faulty washing machine scenario, the question is whether the machine was brought into conformity with the contract when the first attempt at repair was made. Under section 48A(3) there is a presumption that any fault which manifests itself during the first six months was present when the goods were sold. Therefore, it is assumed that Fault 2 was always present, albeit that it was latent. When the repairer came to fix Fault 1, they failed to repair Fault 2 which was an existing (latent) defect. It follows that the trader failed to bring the machine into conformity with the contract. Thus, it might be argued that the consumer is entitled to rescind without first asking for Fault 2 to be repaired.

---

[33]   CSD, Art 3(3), implemented by SoGA, s 48C(2).

7.59   Although this conclusion seems to be the inevitable result of the wording of SoGA, it may be considered to operate harshly against the retailer, who is denied the opportunity to repair a fault they did not know existed. Most jurisdictions around Europe allow for more than one repair by retailers, even in relation to a single fault.[34]

Disproportionate costs – comparing alternative remedies

7.60   One of the implementing measures in the UK departs from the practice in other European states. This is the test to determine whether a seller is obliged to repair or replace goods as demanded by a consumer. In the UK the seller is allowed to compare the proportionality of the request with the other CSD remedies.[35] Thus the seller is not obliged to repair or replace the item if it would be cheaper to rescind the contract. Elsewhere the proportionality of the request may only be compared with the other first tier remedy of repair or replacement. A retailer who is unable to replace the goods is obliged to repair them, however disproportionate the cost of repair may be.

7.61   The differences have occurred as a result of ambiguity within the CSD, and the UK approach appears to have been accepted by the European Commission.[36] Some object to the approach taken, seeing it as stacking the cards in favour of the seller[37] and others have suggested that point needs to be clarified.[38]

Whether the six-month reverse burden begins again

7.62   Section 48A(3) of SoGA states that:

> … goods which do not conform to the contract of sale at any time within the period of six months starting with the date on which the goods were delivered to the buyer must be taken not to have so conformed at that date.

7.63   The section continues by setting out two situations in which this presumption does not apply. Where the seller can show that the goods did conform at the date of delivery, or where the presumption is incompatible with the goods or the fault, the seller is not liable.

7.64   Normally, the relevant "delivery" would be the point at which goods are first delivered to the consumer. The question arises, however, as to whether the redelivery of repaired goods, or the delivery of replacement goods, acts so as to restart the six-month reverse burden of proof. Does a redelivery qualify as a relevant delivery?

---

[34]   With Poland as an exception: see Study Group on a European Civil Code, *Principles of European Law on Sales* Art 4:203, note 4.

[35]   SoGA, s 48B(3).

[36]   European Commission Communication COM (2007) 210 final.

[37]   G Howells and S Weatherill, *Consumer Protection Law* (2nd ed 2005) p 201.

[38]   H Schulte-Nölke, C Twigg-Flesner and M Ebers, *EC Consumer Law Compendium - Comparative Analysis* (April 2007), p 668:
http://ec.europa.eu/consumers/cons_int/safe_shop/acquis/comp_analysis_en.pdf.

7.65   SoGA defines delivery as "voluntary transfer of possession from one person to another",[39] which could cover the situation of a redelivery. Elsewhere in Part 5A of SoGA, however, the term is used in a manner that seems inconsistent with this reading. It states that a buyer has to give value for the use of the goods since "delivery".[40]

7.66   *Benjamin's Sale of Goods* argues in favour of restarting the six-month period upon redelivery. This is said to be "consistent with the thrust" of the European approach, though it is recognised that difficult problems may arise if different defects manifest themselves at different times.[41]

7.67   Arguably, the retailer is obliged to provide goods that conform with the contract whenever they repair or replace goods.

CONCLUSION

7.68   Although most stakeholders accept and understand the basic structure of the existing law, there are significant and often unnecessary complexities. These are not just theoretical, but affect standard day to day examples of faulty goods (such as our washing machine scenario). Consumer groups point out that consumers are often put at a disadvantage in asserting their rights because of the uncertainties and difficulties within the law. On the other hand, some consumers over-estimate their rights, causing unnecessary disputes with businesses.

7.69   Consumer law covers a wide variety of different goods, from a sandwich to a new car. It is not always possible to make the law simple and clear cut if it is to cover the full range of possible cases. However, we have identified the following areas where simplification or clarification is needed:

    (1)   How long is a reasonable time to reject goods? This is often crucial, but it is difficult to draw any firm conclusions from the case law.

    (2)   There are different burdens of proof, depending on whether a consumer is asking for a refund or a repair or replacement. This causes unnecessary confusion.

    (3)   Consumers benefit from the CSD presumption that goods are faulty at the time of sale if the fault appears within six months, but it is not clear whether the six-month period restarts after a repair or replacement.

    (4)   Consumers do not understand the difference between the right to reject and rescission. They also resent the idea of giving an allowance for use, especially after a series of lengthy delays.

    (5)   The different remedies applying to non-sale supply contracts may cause confusion.

[39]   SoGA, s 61(1).

[40]   SoGA, s 48C(3), quoted in para 8.147 below.

[41]   *Benjamin's Sale of Goods* (7th ed 2006) para 12-087. R Bradgate and C Twigg-Flesner, *Blackstone's Guide to Consumer Sales and Associated Guarantees* (2003) p 97 agrees that it would be "common sense" to restart the period, but says that this may go against a strict reading of the Directive.

(6) Both consumer and business groups would welcome more guidance about how to progress from a first tier to a second tier remedy, particularly on what constitutes "a reasonable time" for a repair and "significant inconvenience".

PART 8
PROPOSALS FOR REFORM

INTRODUCTION

8.1 In this Part we discuss possible reforms, ask questions and set out our provisional proposals for consultation.

8.2 We start by considering the right to reject: should it be retained, extended or clarified? We think that it should be retained as a short-term right, but the law should do more to clarify how long it lasts. We provisionally propose that it should normally last for 30 days, but that it should be possible to extend or reduce this period in limited circumstances. Consumers should be entitled to exercise the right to reject for minor defects (such as scratches) which amount to a breach of the implied term as to quality, and should benefit from the reverse burden of proof set out in the Consumer Sales Directive (CSD).

8.3 We then consider whether identical remedies should apply to non-sale contracts. We seek views on whether the law should be harmonised between contracts for sale and those for exchange and for work and materials. We think that different arguments apply to hire contracts and (possibly) hire purchase.

8.4 The next part of the paper is aimed at improving the remedies set out in the CSD. Our provisional proposals are put forward as part of the current debate within the European Union about how the CSD should be reformed. We look both at the CSD itself and at the European Commission's proposal for a new directive on consumer rights, which uses much of the same terminology. As well as forming part of the European debate, it may be possible to implement reforms in the UK only, provided that any replacement to the CSD continues to be a measure requiring only minimum harmonisation.

8.5 We provisionally propose guidance on how many attempts at repair and replacement should be allowed and on best practice in the repair and replacement process. We also think that the CSD should allow consumers to proceed to the second tier remedies when goods are dangerous or the retailer behaves unreasonably. We propose that the remedy of rescission should no longer involve a deduction for use.

8.6 We then look at how the six-month reverse burden of proof applies after a repair or replacement, and at whether remedies should be confined to faults which appear within the first two years. We also consider the remedies appropriate when the seller has delivered the wrong quantity of goods, or has delivered goods late.

8.7 The next section looks at the residual role played by the law on damages, and recommends that this remedy should continue to be available.

8.8 The final sections consider how CSD remedies can be integrated with the right to reject; and the urgent need to improve consumer education in this area.

RETAINING THE RIGHT TO REJECT

8.9 The first question is whether the UK should retain a short-term right to return faulty goods and obtain a refund. The European Commission's proposal for a new directive on consumer rights would require that this traditional remedy is removed, so that the consumer's first recourse would be to ask for a repair or replacement. On this basis, refunds would only be available where there was a problem with providing a repair or replacement.

8.10 In 1987, the two Law Commissions considered the right to reject, and decided that it was important to keep it. We begin by looking at what we said then. We go on to look at the arguments which have been put to us in the course of this review, and how the right operates in other jurisdictions, before reaching a conclusion.

The Law Commissions' 1987 report on the Sale and Supply of Goods

8.11 The Law Commissions published a Consultation Paper in 1983,[1] followed by a Report in 1987.[2] The Consultation Paper recognised that in some cases a consumer may be prepared to accept repair or replacement ("cure"), and this should be encouraged where it is acceptable to both parties. The paper therefore proposed incorporating the notion of cure into the legislation.

8.12 Although this drew some support, two formidable objections emerged. The first was that it would damage consumers' interests by giving retailers grounds to argue that consumers were not entitled to return defective goods and claim back the price. The second was that too many practical questions were left unanswered. For example, how quickly did the "cure" have to be effected? As a consequence, the Law Commissions decided not to recommend a scheme of cure. The Report concluded:

> Although the scheme sounded superficially attractive, when it was exposed to the merciless test of being put into practice, it was likely to prove a breeding ground for dispute and uncertainty, ultimately leading to a more unsatisfactory situation than exists at present and almost certainly being to the detriment of consumers.

8.13 The 1987 Report noted that the right to reject is easy for the non-lawyer to understand and puts the consumer in a strong bargaining position.[3] Once a consumer has had the purchase price returned, they then have a full choice of what goods to buy, from the same or a different supplier. The Law Commissions therefore recommended that a first instance right to reject should be retained.[4]

---

[1] Sale and Supply of Goods (1983) Law Com WP No 85; Scot Law Com CM No 58.

[2] Sale and Supply of Goods (1987) Law Com No 160; Scot Law Com No 104.

[3] A Apps noted that schemes of cure give only a very limited coercive power to the buyer to secure correct performance; and that if the seller has the right to cure it deprives the buyer, at least temporarily, of the right to terminate the contract for breach which is a stronger self-help remedy, and a powerful tool for the buyer. "The Right to Cure Defective Performance" *Lloyds Maritime and Commercial Law Quarterly* [1994] 525 at 555.

[4] Sale and Supply of Goods (1987) Law Com No 160; Scot Law Com No 104, p 39.

The evidence received in the course of this project

8.14 During the course of this project, we have been presented with evidence that the right to reject continues to be valued. The available research shows that people often (in about 20% of cases) take the view that a refund is the appropriate initial remedy, usually because they have lost confidence in the goods or seller.[5] They may perceive the goods as dangerous, or think that the fault will recur, or consider the retailer to be uncooperative. The FDS research shows that consumers feel strongly that they should have a right to reject faulty goods if it is necessary to do so.

8.15 Consumer groups and several academics have emphasised that the right to reject is an essential element which underpins the UK regime. The right to reject strengthens the consumer's bargaining position and has also driven standards up in industry which benefits consumers and businesses alike. For instance, we have been informed that reputable motor dealers undertake a thorough check of cars prior to sale (for example, the "50 point check") to ensure that there are no faults and that cars will not be returned. Furthermore, the right encourages retailers to minimise the inconvenience of repairs by (for example) providing courtesy cars, so that consumers will be prepared to agree to repairs in lieu of exercising the right to reject.

8.16 Several academic writers have argued strongly for the right to reject. In 2003, Ervine described it as particularly important where there has been a lack of confidence in the product:

> The primary remedy for a consumer buyer has been, and continues to be, rejection of the goods. This is a potent but, at least in contracts of sale, a short term weapon as it is a right which is lost, amongst other ways, after the lapse of a reasonable time... Where the defect is such that the consumer has lost confidence in them he or she may well wish to reject the goods and seek another brand rather than explore the new remedies. It might also be the case that a consumer who has these rights will prefer them to the somewhat complex system brought in by the directive.[6]

8.17 Similarly, Willett and others describe the advantages of the right to reject as follows:

---

[5] See FDS research and OFT Report on Consumer Detriment (Parts 4 and 5 and Appendix A of this Consultation Paper).

[6] W C H Ervine, "The Sale and Supply of Goods to Consumers Regulations 2002" 2003 SLT (News) 67 at 69.

There may be cases where immediately upon receipt of goods the consumer may have no confidence that the seller will be able adequately to repair or replace the goods. This may stem from the serious nature of the defect; his knowledge or past experience of the repair or replacement capacities of the seller; or the general attitude of the seller. Based on this lack of confidence, the consumer may wish to reject the goods and terminate the contract immediately, without giving the seller the chance to repair or replace. Another justification for an immediate right to reject or terminate is that such a right may strengthen the bargaining position of the consumer. Most consumer disputes will in practice be resolved (or not resolved) by negotiation with the seller, as the consumer may lack the knowledge, time or resources to go to court. A clear, immediate right to reject the goods strengthens the position of the consumer in trying to persuade the seller to give him what he wants (whether this is in fact a refund, a replacement or simply a speedy repair). If all the consumer wants, in fact, is a quick, no-questions-asked repair, his ability to threaten rejection should provide a good incentive to the seller to agree to do the repair.[7]

8.18   Our discussions with retailers and manufacturers did not find any strong body of opinion that the right to reject should be abolished. Some acknowledged that even if it were abolished, consumers would still expect to be able to obtain refunds for faulty goods, and a mismatch between consumer expectations and the law would lead to disputes. There appeared to be little appetite for radical change.

8.19   Meanwhile consumer groups strongly supported retaining the right to reject. Which? submitted the following example to illustrate its importance:

A consumer purchased a car for approximately £60,000, and waited a year for it to be delivered. Within three weeks of the consumer receiving the car, it caught fire and was severely damaged. The interior and electrics were destroyed and the paintwork extensively damaged as the heat had melted and blistered the paintwork. The consumer rejected the car and the dealer accepted this rejection.

8.20   Which? went on to explain that if the consumer had not had the right to reject there would have been the following consequences:

(1)   The consumer would have been forced to keep a car that they had lost confidence in, not just in terms of this particular car but also the brand and model. Accordingly a replacement car would not have been an acceptable remedy to this consumer.

---

[7]   C Willett, M Morgan-Taylor and A Naidoo, "The Sale and Supply of Goods to Consumers Regulations" [2004] *Journal of Business Law* 94.

(2)   Given the value of the car it could have been economic from the dealer's point of view to carry out a repair. As the repairs would have been extensive, they would have taken some time. Repairs may have been carried out within "a reasonable time" for the purposes of the CSD regime, but still caused the consumer inconvenience, especially if the first repair had been ineffective.

(3)   If repairs were carried out, and the consumer subsequently attempted to sell the car, it is probable that the car would be worth significantly less than the same car without the repair history.

8.21   Which? told us that consumers were particularly concerned about becoming trapped into a cycle of failed repairs, a point which also emerged from the FDS focus groups. Consumers were concerned about the time, trouble and even expense that the repair and replacement process can entail. These include having to return to the shop to collect repaired goods, difficulties diagnosing the cause of faults, delay in repairs, the risk of the fault recurring, and prolonged negotiations or disputes. In some cases, the fact that the goods have been repaired means that they have reduced in value.

The right to reject in other European jurisdictions

8.22   The European Commission has argued that retailers are discouraged from trading across national borders because of the difficulties of coping with a plethora of different regimes. The argument is made that if consumers in other member states are happy to trade on the basis of CSD remedies only, there is no reason why UK consumers would not also find these remedies adequate. We have therefore looked in as much detail as the time allowed at how consumer remedies operate in other member states.[8]

8.23   We found that at least eight European jurisdictions currently have a "right to reject" of some description. This means that consumers have a right to return goods, cancel the contract and obtain a refund for faulty goods as a remedy of first instance in those jurisdictions. In five member states,[9] consumers have the right to exercise a free choice between the four CSD remedies (which means that they can rescind the contract at first instance and obtain money back). In addition, consumers in the UK, Ireland and France have a "right to reject" which exists outside the CSD regime. It is worth noting that other jurisdictions outside Europe, such as the states of the United States and New Zealand, also have a right to reject.

---

[8]   See Appendices C and D, provided on our website at www.lawcom.gov.uk and www.scotlawcom.gov.uk.

[9]   Latvia, Greece, Lithuania, Slovenia and Portugal.

8.24 Furthermore, several other member states did recognise a right to reject before the CSD reforms.[10] It is therefore part of the consumer culture even in jurisdictions where it is no longer recognised in law. Our survey of European Consumer Centres shows that even in member states where no legal right to reject exists, retailers will often offer such a right in practice, recognising that consumers desire such a right.

8.25 The importance of the right to reject and obtain a full refund in certain circumstances is recognised in the Principles of European Law on Sales. The Principles are an attempt to review the law of sales in all the European jurisdictions, and to create a single code that largely mirrors national regimes. Article 4:203(b) of that code permits the buyer to refuse a cure where the buyer has lost confidence in the seller. The example given is of a buyer who orders food for a party but finds a dead mouse in one of the pies.

8.26 Thus there is a fairly strong cultural tradition across Europe that where consumers take home products only to find that they are faulty, they should be entitled to return them and receive a refund. If there is a need to harmonise laws across the EU, there is a strong argument that the harmonised regime should incorporate a right to reject.

Conclusion

8.27 We have come to the conclusion that a short-term right to reject should be retained, for similar reasons to those which we gave in 1987.

8.28 We accept that many consumers will be happy with a repair or a replacement. However, the right to reject inspires consumer confidence. Consumers know that if the good was not as promised, they can return it and get their money back, provided they act quickly. This makes them more prepared to try unknown brands or new retailers.

8.29 Consumers value the right to reject, because it provides them with a remedy where they have lost trust in the product or the retailer. It is an important bargaining tool which prevents buyers becoming trapped in a cycle of failed repairs. It therefore drives up standards, both by encouraging retailers to check products before they are sold and to make the repair process as painless as possible. Furthermore, it is simple and relatively easy for consumers to understand.

[10] See further para 6.5 above.

8.30 Many retailers, in the UK and in other jurisdictions, have voluntary policies which permit consumers to obtain refunds for faulty goods. However, we do not think that the consumer's right to a refund for faulty goods should be left merely to retailers' voluntary policies. Such policies are often confusing. Not only are there wide variations among them but, as voluntary marketing tools, their terms can and do change from time to time. It is also possible that a retailer might withdraw its policy entirely. We think that the right to a refund if goods are faulty is sufficiently important to be enshrined in law. It would be quite unsatisfactory if the fundamental basis of consumers' rights were not a legal right; that is demanded by the principle of the rule of law. That law should be clear, reflect good market practice, and match consumers' legitimate expectations.

8.31 **We provisionally propose that the right to reject should be retained as a short-term remedy of first instance for consumers**.

SHOULD THE RIGHT TO REJECT BE EXTENDED?

8.32 The Sale of Goods Act 1979 (SoGA) currently favours finality, as the right to reject is a short-term remedy. In 1987, the Law Commissions concluded that this was the correct approach – they did not favour a long-term right to reject. One reason was the difficulty of accounting for interim use. Consumers who exercise the right to reject a product may recover the full purchase price, notwithstanding that they have enjoyed some use from it.[11] This differs from the European remedy for "rescission", where some member states provide that a deduction can be made for the use the consumer has had from the product.[12]

8.33 The Law Commissions were concerned that, in many cases, it would not be fair to retailers to allow a long-term right to reject goods without giving some form of credit for use and enjoyment. This raises difficult problems of calculation which would take away much of the force of the remedy of the right to reject. It is likely that the consumer would become involved in argument or negotiation.

8.34 The Law Commissions thought that a long-term right to reject might create other problems. Retailers would suspect that the reasons for return were not genuine, and that the consumer had had the use they wanted or simply changed their mind about a purchase. They were also persuaded that a long-term right would have a significant effect on the retail industry in that the cost to retailers would increase and such cost would be passed on to consumers in increased prices.

8.35 In 1990, Mullan argued that the Law Commissions had been wrong to rule out a long-term right to reject.[13] In contemporary terms, and in the context of the CSD regime, a long-term right to reject might effectively mean giving consumers a free choice between repair, replacement, rejection ("rescission") or reduction in price, whenever the right was exercised. This possibility was also raised in the review of the consumer acquis.[14]

---

[11] See *Benjamin's Sale of Goods* (7th ed 2006) para 12-068.

[12] SoGA, s 48C(3). Recital 15 CSD.

[13] K Mullan, "Satisfaction guaranteed or no deal" [1990] *Journal of Business Law* 231 at 238.

[14] European Commission, *Green Paper on the Consumer Acquis* COM (2006) 744 final, para 5.7.2.

8.36 We have therefore considered whether the right should be extended so that, for example, consumers could return goods when latent defects became apparent several months (or possibly years) after purchase.

The arguments for and against extension

8.37 The main argument for extension is that it would provide an appropriate remedy for latent defects. It is now accepted that goods should be durable. This is a factor to consider when assessing whether goods meet the implied term of satisfactory quality.[15] If a washing machine functions well for six months, but then breaks down, there may be a breach of the implied term as to quality. However, the right to reject will almost certainly have been lost due to lapse of time. The consumer will be left with only the CSD remedies or damages.

8.38 There are situations where the law does recognise a long-term right to reject. For example, in exchange or work and material contracts, the common law doctrine of affirmation applies. This means that consumers do not lose the right to reject until they learn of the defect.[16] Similarly, in Ireland, the buyer is deemed only to accept goods "when without good and sufficient reason, he retains the goods without intimating to the seller that he has rejected them".[17] The fact that a defect was latent, and took a while to be discovered, would be a good and sufficient reason for the delay.

8.39 On the other hand, we think the arguments put to the Law Commissions in 1987 continue to be persuasive. A long-term right could be abused by consumers who have had the use they wanted from the product (for example, by returning an expensive outfit immediately after a wedding). This would increase costs, and therefore prices. Earlier this year, retailers reiterated these views to us. They still do not favour a long-term right to reject, and are keen to be able to "close their books" after a relatively short period of time.

8.40 The right to reject is a powerful weapon but we think that it should be kept for faults which manifest themselves immediately or after a short period of use. After the product has been used for a while, the primary remedy should be a repair or replacement. Under our proposals, retailers would be free to agree to extend the period if they thought that there was a competitive advantage in doing so.

8.41 **We provisionally conclude that the right to reject should not be extended to cover latent defects which appear only after a prolonged period of use.**

---

[15] SoGA, s 14(2B)(e).

[16] In Scotland, an equivalent result is achieved through the operation of personal bar. Personal bar cannot operate until the consumer knows of the defect.

[17] Sale of Goods Act 1893, s 35(c), as amended by the (Irish) Sale of Goods and Supply of Services Act 1980.

CLARIFYING THE RIGHT TO REJECT

8.42 As discussed in Part 7, the main problem with the right to reject is uncertainty over how long it lasts. This adds complexity and difficulty to what is intended to be a simple and certain bargaining tool. It is difficult for consumer advisers to give guidance, or for shop staff to understand what the law requires. We have therefore considered whether the concept of a reasonable time should be replaced by a fixed period, after which the right to reject is automatically lost.

The 1987 report

8.43 Again, the Law Commissions considered this issue in 1987 and rejected a fixed period as unworkable.[18] The periods suggested at the time ranged from 14 days to 12 months. The report concluded that the enormous variety of goods made it impossible to set a fixed time.

8.44 The Law Commissions thought that a fixed time would be arbitrary. No single time limit would be appropriate for all the wide variety of goods and circumstances and the result could be unreasonable or even absurd. Similarly, it would be impractical to set different time periods for different goods, because the different categories (however carefully defined) would inevitably create borderline cases where it was not clear into which category a product fell. Any fixed period would also remove the flexibility inherent in allowing the right to reject to be exercised within "a reasonable time", which is beneficial for fairness. The 1987 Report concluded:

> We are, of course, well aware that the concept of a "reasonable time" does not provide a certain answer which can be applied in every case. No one on consultation was, however, able to offer a better solution than at present…. A more rigid provision, if intended to apply to all types of goods, would almost inevitably create certainty at the expense of justice.

As often happens where reform of the law is concerned, a balance has to be struck between certainty and fairness.

The arguments today

8.45 We have considered these arguments again. In 2008, consumers are more used to fixed time periods. For example, most consumers are familiar with high street retailers' "no-quibble money-back guarantees", which are sometimes set at 28 or 30 days. In addition, the CSD states that, for consumer durables, any fault that manifests itself during the first six months is presumed to have been present when the goods were sold.

8.46 In our discussions with stakeholders, there was some support for fixing a time limit at around a month. The main advantage is that the law would be easier to enforce informally. The clear time limit set in legislation could be quoted in disputes.

---

[18] Sale and Supply of Goods (1987) Law Com No 160; Scot Law Com No 104, p 47.

8.47 However, most stakeholders indicated that there should still be room for exceptions; otherwise the law might operate too harshly. For example, in the FDS consumer groups, almost everyone thought that if a teddy bear bought as a Christmas present in October falls apart as soon as it is opened on Christmas day, the consumer should be entitled to a refund. Some goods cannot be tested within the month: for example, a lawnmower bought in November cannot be tested until spring. However, for perishable goods, a month is too long. Consumers should not be given the impression that they can take a month to return sour milk or bad meat. It is important that consumers should return goods in a state where the presence of the fault can still be detected.

8.48 We are also conscious that the original principle behind a reasonable period was to provide the buyer with an opportunity to inspect the goods. This therefore requires some degree of flexibility.

8.49 These arguments are persuasive. We think that the law should provide clear guidance about the normal period for exercising the right to reject goods. However, it should be open to traders to argue for a shorter period in some circumstances, or for consumers to argue for a longer period in other circumstances. Below, we consider the normal period which should be prescribed by law, and the possible reasons for departing from it.

A normal period of 30 days

8.50 We think that the legislation should indicate that in normal circumstances, a consumer should exercise the right to reject goods within 30 days from the date of delivery.

8.51 The rationale for a 30-day period is that it should give the consumer an opportunity to inspect the goods, and to test them for a short period in actual use. So, in the case of clothes, for example, it enables the consumer to do more than simply try the clothes on. The 30-day period is intended to allow enough time to wear the clothes and wash them, and if they fall apart in the wash, return them to the shop. For a washing machine, 30 days should give enough time to install the machine and use the main programmes. For a new computer, it enables the consumer to install the software they intend to use and to test it in practice. For a car, the consumer would have an opportunity to drive in a variety of road conditions, including at night and on the motorway. However, the 30-day period does require the consumer to act promptly. A consumer will lose the right to reject if they just leave their new clothes in the wardrobe for six weeks.

8.52 A secondary reason for choosing a 30-day period is that it appears to correspond with consumers' expectations. When consumers were asked to say how long the right currently lasted, 30 days was the answer most commonly given, probably because consumers have become used to 30-day no-quibble money-back guarantees.[19] Although the right to reject faulty goods is quite different from the right to return non-faulty goods, we think that a 30-day period is one which the public will understand and remember.

---

[19] In the FDS research, two-thirds of consumers estimated that the right to a refund for faulty goods lasts one month (while most of the remaining third thought that it lasts for one year).

8.53   At present, consumer advisers are often concerned about advising consumers that they can reject goods after two or three weeks. If consumer advisers were able to tell people that the standard period was 30 days, it would give consumers greater confidence and reduce the need to rely on ambiguous case law.

Reasons for a shorter period

8.54   We think that in some cases it should be open to the trader to argue that the time to exercise the right to reject should be less than 30 days.

PERISHABLE GOODS

8.55   The main scenario where a shorter time would be appropriate is where the goods are of a type expected to perish within 30 days, so that after 30 days it is no longer possible to tell whether the goods were faulty at the time of purchase. We think that for fresh food the right to reject should last for much less than 30 days.

ACTS INCONSISTENT WITH RETURNING GOODS

8.56   We also think that the onus should be on consumers to inspect goods carefully before they alter them or mingle them with other things. For example, consumers should be required to check the colour of paint before applying it to the wall, or that tiles are the same as the sample before laying them. We think that the legislation should provide that where a consumer has carried out an act which is inconsistent with returning the goods (cutting cloth, altering clothes), the consumer may not reject for a fault which should have been discovered before the inconsistent act.

8.57   On the other hand, we do not wish to suggest that any act which makes goods difficult to resell should prevent consumers from exercising the right to reject. In many cases, the consumer will only be able to discover that the wine is bad after they have opened the bottle, or that a pie contains a dead mouse after they have cut into it. This is a necessary part of the testing process.

8.58   Nor are we convinced that adapting goods should always result in the loss of the right to reject. Suppose, for example, that a consumer shortens trousers, wears them and washes them, and then discovers that they are not colour fast (as stated on the label). If it was unreasonable to expect the consumer to have discovered that the trousers were not as described before altering them, then the consumer may still exercise the right to reject within the 30-day period.

Reasons for a longer time

OBJECTIVE FACTORS

8.59 There are many instances where it is clear to both parties from the nature of the sale that the consumer will not be able to test the goods in use during the next month. Macleod gives the example of skis bought at an end of ski-season sale.[20] When this scenario was discussed in Parliament, it was said that if the skis were left unused in a cupboard for many months, the court should discount that period, so that the reasonable time for exercising the right to reject would be extended.[21] It is also foreseeable that the lawnmower bought in November would not be used until spring. In both examples, we think that there would be a good reason to extend the period beyond 30 days.

8.60 The most common scenario is when Christmas gifts are bought in the autumn. In the FDS research, consumers discussed a scenario in which a teddy bear was bought in October, and fell apart as soon as it was opened on Christmas day. Almost everyone thought that the consumer should be entitled to a refund in this case.[22] In practice, many retailers make some allowance for gifts by allowing a longer period than usual for refunds, or providing "gift receipts" which make special provision for the return of unwanted (including faulty) gifts. We think that if it were reasonably within the contemplation of both parties that the goods would not be opened until Christmas day (for example, toys bought in the pre-Christmas period), the period for exercising the right to reject should be extended.

8.61 Thus we think it should be open to the consumer to argue that at the time of the purchase it was reasonably foreseeable by both parties that a longer period would be needed to inspect the goods and to try them out in practice. In appropriate cases, the extension might be quite lengthy. The skis bought in April, for example, might not be used until the following March. Similarly a lawnmower may remain unused for six months.

AGREEMENT

8.62 In some cases, the seller may specifically agree to extend the period for the right to reject by, for example, providing a gift receipt. Where sellers agree to allow the buyer to test the goods outside the 30-day period, we think that the normal period should be extended.

PERSONAL FACTORS

8.63 In the *Bernstein* case, the judge discounted a few days when the consumer had been ill, on the grounds that he had not had an opportunity to drive his new car during that time. The judge commented

---

[20] J K Macleod, *Consumer Sales Law* (2002) para 29.07.

[21] See above, para 7.29.

[22] See Appendix A.

> I discount the period when the plaintiff was ill because reasonable seems to me to be referable to the individual buyer's situation as well as to that of the seller.[23]

8.64 Subsequent cases have also suggested that the current law should take into account the buyer's personal circumstances, even if the retailer could not foresee them. Examples in case law are a short period of holiday or illness, when the buyer was unable to try out the goods.[24] However, the period allowed for these personal circumstances has typically been short, on the ground that it has to be weighed against what may seem reasonable to the seller.

8.65 We ask whether it should be open to consumers to argue that the period should be extended for longer than 30 days where they have been unable to test the goods for a good reason, for example because they have been ill or on holiday. We think that there should be some element of inability to test goods, rather than it merely being the consumer's choice not to test.

8.66 We think that while objective circumstances may justify a long extension of many months, personal circumstances may justify no more than a few weeks. For example:

> A consumer buys skis in February, intending a ski holiday in March. However, they are then forced to cancel their holiday through illness. The consumer does not go skiing until the following March. As soon as they put their skis on, they break.

8.67 Although from the consumer's point of view it was reasonable to take 13 months to test the goods, this was not foreseeable at the time of sale. Our initial view is that it would be unreasonable from the point of view of the retailer to allow such an extended period. Instead, the consumer should rely on their CSD remedies of repair or replacement. We would welcome views on whether personal factors should justify only a short extension (of a few weeks) or of a longer period (possibly up to six months).

FUNDAMENTAL DEFECTS WHICH TAKE TIME TO DISCOVER

8.68 We have already explained that the right to reject should not be extended to cover latent defects which appear only after a prolonged period of use. This raises the question, however, whether the period for the right to reject should be extended where it takes time for fundamental faults to be discovered.

---

[23] [1987] 2 All ER 220 at 231.

[24] See for example, Judge Raymond Jack's statement in *Truk (UK) Ltd v Tokmakidis GmbH* [2000] 2 All ER (Comm) 594 that the reasonable period should bear in mind both the buyer's and the seller's position. See above, para 3.39.

8.69 An example would be where a consumer buys seeds for a particularly rare and valuable heirloom plant. The consumer plants the seeds, but when they grow they turn out to be standard hybrids. The question is whether the consumer should be entitled to receive a refund of the price paid, or should be required to accept a replacement. The argument for allowing a refund is that the goods were never as described. In effect the consumer has been sold something quite different to that which they intended to buy, but had no immediate means of discovering the problem. The failure is so fundamental that the consumer should be entitled to their money back. If the consumer accepts a replacement, the new seeds will take another six months to grow and the consumer may have lost confidence that the replacements will be as described.

8.70 The alternative argument is that this is the same as any other serious latent defect which takes time to discover. It should therefore be dealt with under a reformed CSD scheme. As we discuss later, we think that the consumer should not be required to accept a repair or replacement where the seller has forfeited the buyer's trust, but should be entitled to proceed straight to rescission.

8.71 Although we anticipate that this problem may not arise very often, we would nevertheless welcome consultees' views on this point.

The length of time

8.72 We have considered three different periods of time which the normal period should be presumed to be: six weeks, 30 days, or three weeks.

8.73 A period of 30 days appears to be in line with consumer expectations. In the FDS research, two-thirds of consumers estimated that the right to a refund for faulty goods lasts one month (while the remaining third thought that it lasts for one year). As we have said above, a 30-day period tallies with many no-quibble money-back guarantees, so is already in retailers' and the public's consciousness with regard to returns.

8.74 We think it would improve the current position, where consumer advisers are often concerned about advising consumers that they can reject goods after two or three weeks. If consumer advisers were able to give a standard period of 30 days, this would provide the desired guidance for most consumers, and reduce the need to rely on ambiguous case law.

8.75 **We provisionally propose that the legislation should set out a normal 30-day period during which consumers should exercise their right to reject. The 30-day period should run from date of purchase, delivery or completion of contract, whichever is later.**

8.76 **Do consultees agree that 30 days is an appropriate period? We would be interested in receiving arguments for either a shorter or longer period.**

8.77 **Do consultees think that:**

    (1) **it should it be open to the retailer to argue for a shorter period where**

(a)   **the goods are perishable (that is they are by their nature expected to perish within 30 days)?**

(b)   **the consumer should have discovered the fault before carrying out an act inconsistent with returning goods?**

(2)   **it should it be open to the consumer to argue for a longer period where**

(a)   **it was reasonably foreseeable at the time of sale that a longer period would be needed ("objective circumstances")?**

(b)   **the parties agreed to extend the period?**

(c)   **the consumer's personal circumstances made it impossible to examine the goods within the 30-day period? If so, should this justify only a short extension, such as an additional 30 days, or a longer extension of six months or more?**

(d)   **there were fundamental defects which took time to be discovered?**

(3)   **there are other reasons to justify a shorter or longer period?**

THE REVERSE BURDEN OF PROOF AND THE RIGHT TO REJECT

8.78   Under the CSD, durable goods are presumed to be faulty at the time of the sale if the fault appears within six months of delivery. Thus if a fault appears within six months of delivery it is up to the retailer to show that the goods were not faulty at the time of delivery. However, the reverse burden does not apply if the consumer is seeking a domestic remedy.

8.79   Commentators have suggested that, in the interests of simplicity, the reverse burden of proof should also apply to domestic remedies. Currently, there is little awareness amongst consumers that there are different burdens of proof. Willett and others wrote:

> This six-month presumption is to be welcomed from the point of view of consumer protection. There is more chance that sellers will have access to information which will help to establish that goods are in conformity than there is that consumers will have access to information needed to establish non-conformity at the time of sale. Although it was not required by the Directive, it seems unfortunate that this six-month presumption was not applied to the pre-existing remedies, ie the short-term right to reject and the right to claim damages.[25]

---

[25]   C Willett, M Morgan-Taylor and A Naidoo, "The Sale and Supply of Goods to Consumers Regulations" [2004] *Journal of Business Law* 94.

8.80 We suspect that, at least in terms of the right to reject, an extension of the six-month reverse burden to domestic remedies would not lead to any great practical change. Usually as a matter of common sense people accept that a fault which appears within 30 days was present at the time of sale, unless there is a reason to think that it was not present. The benefits of this change would be simplicity, and better integration of the CSD remedies with domestic remedies.

8.81 **We provisionally propose that a consumer who exercises a right to reject should be entitled to a reverse burden of proof that the fault was present when the goods were delivered.**

THE RIGHT TO REJECT FOR "MINOR" DEFECTS

8.82 Under current law, once a consumer has shown that one of the implied terms of quality has been breached,[26] they may exercise the right to reject, provided they have not accepted the goods. There is no exclusion for minor defects.

8.83 This differs from Article 3(6) of the CSD, which states that "the consumer is not entitled to have the contract rescinded if the lack of conformity is minor." At present, the UK, amongst other member states, has not implemented that provision. However, under the European Commission's proposals, this would change. Member states would no longer be permitted to allow consumers to rescind a contract for minor defects. The only remedies for minor defects would be repair, replacement or a reduction in price.

8.84 Again, this was one of the issues considered by the Law Commissions in 1987. At the time there was doubt about the extent to which the implied term as to quality in SoGA covered "minor" defects, such as minor imperfections in appearance, finish or functioning.

8.85 The 1987 Report noted that consumers often cared a great deal about the appearance and finish of new consumer goods such as cars, white goods and clothing. It concluded that in appropriate cases the consumer is entitled to expect that the goods will be free from even small imperfections. Consequently, the Report recommended that the new definition of quality should specifically refer to appearance, finish, and freedom from minor defects. The law was amended to this effect in 1994, to indicate that the existence of minor defects is a relevant factor in determining whether goods meet the required standard of quality.[27]

8.86 The 1987 Report also concluded that consumers should have the right to reject where the existence of blemishes and other minor defects led to the implied term being breached. An exception for minor defects would lead to unnecessary disputes. Furthermore, damages would be unlikely to be a satisfactory remedy:

---

[26] In Scotland, the breach must be material: SoGA, s 15B(1)(b). In a consumer contract, however, breach of any term as to the quality of the goods or their fitness for a purpose, or any term that the goods will correspond with a description or sample, is deemed to be a material breach: SoGA, s 15B(2).

[27] SoGA, s 14(2B).

> Even if compensation were agreed, this would often still not be an adequate remedy for the consumer. What he wanted was goods of the proper quality at the full price, not defective goods at a lower price.[28]

8.87   In 2008, it is evident that the appearance of goods is as important (if not more important) to consumers. In many cases consumers spend a great deal of time selecting goods specifically because of their appearance, and pay more for goods because of their appearance. It is appropriate, therefore, that dents, scratches and blemishes will often be breaches of the implied term as to quality. In these cases, a repair or replacement may not be possible or practical, and the consumer will not want a reduction in price because they have selected the goods for their appearance and paid for a specific appearance.

8.88   This point emerged strongly from the research carried out by FDS.[29] When participants were asked what remedy they would expect in the case of a scratched table, most were very reluctant to consider keeping an item which did not look good. They gave many examples of carefully choosing kettles or other kitchen equipment to match their décor. They would not want to keep products which were discoloured or which did not match the sample in the shop.

8.89   We are also concerned that an exception for minor defects would lead to unnecessary disputes. We understand that the question of what constitutes a "minor" defect is problematic in at least some member states which have exercised the option to provide that rescission cannot be exercised in the case of "minor" defects.

8.90   It is our view that the law relating to minor defects should not be changed. That is, it should continue to be possible for consumers to exercise their right to reject, or rescind contracts (under the CSD) for minor defects in appropriate cases.

8.91   **We provisionally propose that legal protection for consumers who purchase goods with "minor" defects should not be reduced.**

THE RIGHT TO REJECT IN OTHER SUPPLY CONTRACTS

8.92   As we have seen, the law currently makes distinctions between sales and other contracts to supply goods, such as work and materials contracts, exchange, hire and hire purchase. For non-sales contracts, the right to reject is not lost by acceptance. Instead, it is more favourable to the consumer. In England and Wales, it continues until the contract has been "affirmed", which can only be done once the consumer is aware of the breach. In Scotland, the right to reject is lost when the consumer, through words or conduct, waives the right to reject the goods.

---

[28]   Sale and Supply of Goods (1987) Law Com No 160; Scot Law Com No 104, p 37.

[29]   See Appendix A.

96

8.93　Below we consider whether this should be changed. Should the sales regime apply equally to other supply contracts? This would mean that consumers may not normally reject goods after the 30-day period has expired. Alternatively, should consumers continue to have a longer period to reject goods when they enter into other supply contracts? We think the arguments differ between contracts where property passes (work and materials and exchange contracts) and those where property does not pass, such as hire and (possibly) hire purchase contracts. We look at each in turn.

8.94　As currently drafted, the European Commission's proposal for a directive on consumer rights would appear to cover contracts for work and materials. These areas would therefore be subject to maximum harmonisation. However, member states would be free to provide their own remedies for breaches of exchange, hire and hire purchase contacts.

Contracts where property passes

Arguments for a uniform regime

8.95　The differences between a contract of sale and one involving work and materials or exchange can be highly technical. It is difficult to know, for example, whether a contract to supply a washing machine as part of a fitted kitchen is best analysed as an all-in-one contract for work and materials, or as a separate, severable, contract for the sale of the washing machine. Similarly, part-exchange deals may be analysed in many different ways. If a consumer trades in their old car in exchange for another second hand car, this might be analysed as two separate sales or as a non-sale exchange contract.

8.96　Even once the type of contract has been correctly analysed, the difference between acceptance and affirmation (or waiver in Scotland) is in many cases too complex for consumers and retailers to understand. Some consumer advisers struggle with the difference, and some lawyers have problems with it. In the *Jones* case, it appeared to cause problems even for the Court of Appeal.[30] Greater simplicity in the law would help both retailers and consumers to understand their rights and resolve their disputes.

8.97　Furthermore, there is no particular reason for treating defects in a car differently simply because a consumer exchanged a previous model. The essential nature of the defect is the same, whether the consumer paid in money or in some other way. Similarly, when a washing machine goes wrong, the fact that the trader also remodelled the consumer's kitchen is not necessarily relevant to the nature of the relationship or the fault.

Arguments for the current law

8.98　On the other hand, consumer groups told us that the law on affirmation or waiver greatly benefits consumers in particularly problematic areas. Work and materials contracts tend to be expensive, usually involving the consumer's home. Typically, they are for double glazing or fitted kitchens or other home improvements. As we saw in Part 5, these products are particularly likely to lead to disputes.

---

[30] *Jones v Gallagher (trading as Gallery Kitchens and Bathrooms)* [2004] EWCA Civ 10; [2005] 1 Lloyd's Reports 377. See the discussion at paras 3.44 to 3.46.

8.99   In work and materials contracts, defects may take time to come to light, and when they do the consumer is particularly likely to lose confidence in the goods or the trader. The other available remedies (claims for damages and first tier CSD remedies of repair or replacement) may not offer satisfactory solutions to the consumer, as they generally require the consumer to allow the trader one or more attempts at repair or replacement. Consumer groups therefore argued that abolishing the doctrine of affirmation or waiver and replacing it with a short-term right to reject would be a significant reduction in consumer rights.

8.100   Furthermore, in work and materials contracts, goods are often selected by the trader, with little input from the consumer. It could be argued that a trader who sells their expertise in selecting and installing goods should bear greater responsibility if they go wrong.

8.101   In 1987, the Law Commissions concluded that the existing rules should be kept. The Consultation Paper commented that:

> A very strong case would have to be made out for removing from the customer part of his existing legal rights.[31]

There was little comment on this proposal and among those who did comment no agreement emerged.

8.102   In the end, the Law Commissions concluded that a change in the law would deprive consumers of the benefits of the current regime and would substitute the less favourable rules of SoGA. The Law Commissions were not aware that there was any particular difficulty in practice about this area of the law and therefore felt that no change was necessary.[32] They argued that a pattern of rights and duties had grown up and the pattern should not be disturbed without compelling reasons to do so.

Conclusion

8.103   In this project, the Law Commissions have not reached a concluded view. On the one hand, our aim is to simplify the law – and removing the distinction between sales and other contracts where property in goods is transferred would be a significant simplification. However, we would welcome views on how far the existing rules provide an important safeguard for consumers.

8.104   **We ask consultees whether the normal 30-day period for rejecting goods should also apply to other contracts for the supply of goods in which property is transferred, or whether the current law should be retained.**

---

[31]   Sale and Supply of Goods (1983) Law Com WP No 85; Scot Law Com CM No 58, p 104.

[32]   Sale and Supply of Goods (1987) Law Com No 160; Scot Law Com No 104, p 55.

Hire contracts

8.105 We think hire contracts are different. In contracts of pure hire there is a continuing relationship between the parties. The goods still belong to the owner who (under the terms of the hire contract) may be under an obligation to repair or replace the hired goods if they break down. The hirer is entitled to expect that the goods will remain in a satisfactory state throughout the period of hire. As Mullan has pointed out:

> Courts appear to conclude that such a continuing interest carries with it an obligation to ensure that goods are of satisfactory quality for the duration of the agreement.[33]

8.106 Furthermore, in hire contracts, there is a convenient method of valuing use – the rate of hire itself can be taken as a basis for the valuation. Finally, the CSD rights do not apply to hire contracts, making the right to terminate the consumer's main remedy.

8.107 All these factors mean that when goods develop a fault, it makes sense for the consumer to terminate the contract, paying for past hire but not future hire. This appears to be the current law and we do not see any reason to change it. We do not think that it causes confusion, but represents what most consumers would expect.

8.108 **We provisionally propose that in hire contracts, the current law should be preserved. When goods develop a fault, the consumer should be entitled to terminate the contract, paying for past hire but not future hire.**

Hire purchase

8.109 In the course of this review, we received little evidence about hire purchase contracts. We understand that whilst this form of credit financing is not as popular as it once was in consumer transactions, it is still used in certain sectors, such as car sales, and the purchase of household appliances and goods.

8.110 In traditional hire purchase agreements, the transaction operated economically as a form of sale. The consumer's primary aim was to acquire ownership of the good, albeit on credit. On this view, it would make sense to treat hire purchase contracts in the same way as other supply contracts where property passes. However, hire purchase is sometimes used primarily as a form of hire, where the option to acquire ownership at the end of the period is hardly ever exercised.

8.111 We have no concluded view on whether hire purchase should be treated as a supply contract to transfer property in goods, or as analogous to a hire contract. We would welcome views.

8.112 **We welcome views on the issues raised by hire purchase contracts, and whether they cause any problems in practice. In particular should hire purchase be treated as a supply contract to transfer property in goods, or as analogous to a hire contract?**

---

[33] K Mullan, "Satisfaction guaranteed or no deal" [1990] *Journal of Business Law* 231.

REFORMING THE CSD

8.113 During the course of this review, stakeholders repeatedly told us that guidance on the operation of the CSD is required. In particular, there is a need to clarify how a buyer moves from first tier to second tier remedies and what amounts to "unreasonable delay" and "significant inconvenience". The issue of deduction for use also causes problems.

8.114 In Part 6 we describe the responses from European Consumer Centres (ECC) about how other member states deal with these questions. These show that other member states are experiencing similar problems of interpretation. As consumer disputes tend to be low value, it is unlikely that these issues will be clarified in case law, either by national courts or the European Court of Justice.

8.115 We welcome the opportunity provided by the review of the consumer acquis to address these issues. The European Commission has made some suggestions for reform in their proposed new directive on consumer rights. In particular, it has proposed to abolish the deduction for use. It also proposes to allow consumers to proceed to a second tier remedy where the trader has implicitly or explicitly refused to remedy the lack of conformity or where the same defect has reappeared more than once within a short period of time.

8.116 In our view, further reform and guidance is needed. We think that most problems are best tackled at a European level in a new directive to replace the CSD. It might, however, also be helpful if further explanation were given at a national level in codes of guidance.

A cycle of failed repairs

8.117 Consumers are particularly concerned about becoming locked into a cycle of failed repairs. This is because it is difficult to know what amounts to a "significant inconvenience" or to an "unreasonable time" for repairs and replacement, entitling the consumer to proceed to the second tier remedies. Which? submitted an example of a case which illustrates that the question of numerous repairs can prove to be a problem under the CSD regime:

> A car was purchased for more than £30,000. The car developed an electrical fault which meant that control of certain functions of the car was lost. The windows would open without warning, which made it difficult to leave the car parked.
>
> Sometimes the effects were more serious. Once the electrical fault caused the engine to start and the car lurched forward whilst parked. Another time the car accelerated to 60 mph without warning. The consumer had to drive the car into a lay-by and apply the brakes while the wheels continued to spin at 60 mph.
>
> As a result of a total loss of confidence in the car, the consumer was unable to drive it and was forced to cancel a holiday. The dealer refused the consumer's attempt to reject the car, on the ground that the consumer was out of time. Instead, the dealer was prepared to carry out repairs to the car. After each repair, initially the problems appeared to have been corrected, but would then return soon after.

The consumer became locked in to a cycle of failed repairs. Each time remedial work was carried out it was done quickly and efficiently and within a reasonable time, and so in practice each repair in isolation could not be said to have caused significant inconvenience; as such it is questionable that the right to rescind was triggered. Ultimately, the consumer purchased another car while the faulty car remained in his garage for approximately 2 years.

8.118 Which? thought that consumers would benefit from clarity about the effect of a series of unsuccessful repairs which were nevertheless carried out efficiently. Which? thought that cumulatively they may amount to "significant inconvenience", even if each one was reasonable when looked at in isolation.

Moving to the second tier

"Reasonable time" and "significant inconvenience"

8.119 In order to rely on the second tier rights of rescission or a reduction in price, the consumer will normally have to show that the seller has failed to carry out a repair or provide a replacement "within a reasonable time and without significant inconvenience".[34] The CSD says that this should take into account "the nature of the goods and the purpose for which the consumer required the goods".[35]

8.120 The questions of the reasonableness of the time and the significance of the inconvenience are questions of fact. Examples of the extremes can easily be given. For instance, a trader would clearly be in breach of its obligations if a family had to manage without a washing machine for months. But the family would probably desire a repair within a day. Between these poles, there is room for debate about what a reasonable time and significant inconvenience means, and these concepts could probably never be defined comprehensively. This represents a real problem in practice, as every case has potential for dispute, arguments and dissatisfaction.

8.121 The CSD states that the purpose for which the consumer required the goods will affect the reasonable time period and the level of inconvenience. Thus the consumer's circumstances can affect the trader's obligations, and there is a necessary element of subjectivity. If, for example, a consumer purchases a fridge for storing insulin, the consumer would be entitled to demand a very rapid replacement. Similarly, a family with young children is entitled to expect their washing machine to be repaired more quickly than a single person would in similar circumstances.

8.122 Whether the consumer bought the product for a specific event could also be important. As Ervine put it:

[34] SoGA, s 48C(2).

[35] CSD, Art 3(3).

If the defective product were, say, a wedding dress or video camera intended to film the wedding, the reference to the purpose for which the product was required might indicate that replacement would take priority over repair if repair could not be effected in time for the event.[36]

8.123 Thus relevant factors in balancing a reasonable time for repairs against the consumer's significant inconvenience include: whether the item was purchased for a special event (for example, a camera bought for a wedding); whether the consumer has a special need for the goods (for example, a fridge for insulin); and whether an item is used daily (such as a washing machine for a young family).

How many repairs?

8.124 A particular problem is how many repairs the consumer must allow before asking for the contract to be rescinded. The CSD defines a repair as "bringing consumer goods into conformity with the contract of sale".[37] SoGA adopts a very similar definition.[38]

8.125 It could be argued that if a fault develops after the trader has made one attempt at repair, the trader is in breach of its obligations because the goods were not brought into conformity with the contract. As a result the consumer is entitled to move on to the second tier remedies.[39] In practice, however, most jurisdictions in Europe allow for the possibility (in theory at least) of more than one repair by a retailer.[40] There is no consensus in Europe about the number of repairs. ECC responses to our questionnaire ranged from one attempt per item to three attempts per fault.

8.126 The European Commission has addressed the problem in its proposal for a directive on consumer rights. It has proposed a new provision which would allow the consumer to rescind the contract or ask for a reduction in price where "the same defect has reappeared more than once within a short period of time".[41] We are concerned that this provides considerable scope for dispute over whether a fault is the same or different from the previous fault, and what constitutes a short period of time.

8.127 Our own view, based upon the ECC responses to our questionnaire and our discussions with stakeholders, is that two attempts (in total, regardless of the number of faults) seems to be a reasonable approach in most situations.

---

[36] W C H Ervine, "The Sale and Supply of Goods to Consumers Regulations 2002" 2003 SLT (News) 67 at 69.

[37] Art 1(2)(f).

[38] SoGA, s 61(1).

[39] In Part 7 we suggest that the way the CSD is worded might suggest that this applies whether it is the same fault or a different fault. However, we conclude that this may be considered to operate too harshly against the retailer – see para 7.59.

[40] With Poland as an exception: see Study Group on a European Civil Code, *Principles of European Law on Sales* Art 4:203, note 4.

[41] Proposal for a directive on consumer rights, art 26(4)(d).

8.128   We think it would be useful to provide a cut off to the effect that after two failed repairs the consumer has a right to rescind the contract. This would prevent the problem where the consumer is trapped in a cycle of repairs, with each further repair seemingly reasonable when looked at in isolation.

8.129   This does not mean that a retailer would always be allowed two repairs. Where an item is in daily use, one failed repair would normally be enough to allow the consumer to rescind the contract. However, a further repair might be reasonable if the retailer had taken steps to reduce the inconvenience by, for example, offering a temporary replacement. In addition, there are certain goods which people rely on, such as wheelchairs, stair lifts, and hearing aids, the absence of which must, by their very nature, lead to significant inconvenience. For such essential items a repair might be unsuitable unless a suitable loan item were provided.

How many replacements?

8.130   The FDS research and feedback from consumer groups universally indicates that most consumers will only accept one attempt at replacement. In our kettle example, once two elements had failed, consumers would conclude that there was a design or quality control problem with the product and want their money back. This is also the usual practice amongst other member states according to our ECC survey.

8.131   We think that consumers should be entitled to rescind the contract if a fault develops in a replacement product.

The form guidance should take

8.132   Some issues can be clarified within a new directive to replace the CSD. For example, we think it would be helpful to insert a provision stating that a consumer should be entitled to rescind the contract after two failed repairs or one failed replacement.

8.133   Other issues may be better dealt with through a provision which gives guidance about what consumers and retailers are entitled to expect but which allows more room for discretion to suit the particular circumstances. We would welcome views on the appropriate form of such guidance.

8.134 One possibility would be to insert examples into the recitals set out in the preamble to the new directive. These do not have legal force but courts do take them into account in ascertaining the purpose of the directive and clarifying the meaning of certain words.[42] Another might be to add a schedule to the new directive along the lines of schedule 2 to the Directive on Unfair Terms in Consumer Contracts 1993.[43] This sets out an indicative and non-exhaustive list of terms which may be regarded as unfair. Alternatively, it might be more appropriate if such guidance were provided at national level. If so, it might be developed by us or by BERR, in consultation with industry and consumer groups.

8.135 **We provisionally propose that the directive which replaces the CSD should state that after two failed repairs, or one failed replacement, the consumer is entitled to proceed to a second tier remedy.**

8.136 **We provisionally propose that further guidance should be provided stating that the consumer should be entitled to rescind the contract:**

(1)   where the product is in daily use, after one failed repair; or

(2)   where the product is essential, immediately;

unless the retailer has reduced the inconvenience to the consumer by, for example, offering a temporary replacement.

8.137 **We welcome views on the form such guidance should take.**

Best practice guidance on the repair and replacement process

8.138 It would also be helpful if there were best practice guidance to address common problem areas. For example, it would be helpful to state that the retailer should use best endeavours to:

(1)   estimate how long it will take for repairs to be carried out;

(2)   keep the consumer informed of material developments, including information about the nature of the fault;

(3)   provide reliable appointment times; and

(4)   keep appointments.

---

[42] The European Court of Justice has held that "the preamble to a Community act has no binding legal force and cannot be relied on as a ground for derogating from the actual provisions of the act in question." Case C-162/97 *Gunnar Nilsson, Per Olov Hagelgren and Solweig Arrborn* [1998] ECR I-7477, at [54]. See also Opinion of A-G Tizzano in Case C-173/99 *R v Sec of State for Trade and Industry ex p BECTU* [2001] ECR I-4881, at [39].

[43] Directive 93/13/EEC.

8.139 A frequent question is whether a retailer should offer compensation for missed appointments and delays. For example, if a consumer with a faulty washing machine experiences three missed appointments, spends £40 at the launderette, loses three mornings' work, and makes repeated telephone calls to the retailer's call centres at a cost of £15, should the consumer be entitled to compensation? This point is discussed again below.[44]

8.140 Again, we welcome views on the form such a best practice code might take. In particular, should it be issued at EU or national level?

8.141 **We provisionally propose that there should be best practice guidance on the process of repairing and replacing goods under the CSD (or any replacement to the CSD).**

8.142 **We ask consultees what form that guidance should take. In particular, should it be issued at EU or national level?**

Other reasons to proceed to second tier remedies

8.143 Consumers felt strongly that they should be able to return goods and receive a refund where they had lost confidence in the product or the retailer. The European Commission has proposed the addition of a provision that the consumer may proceed to a second tier remedy where "the trader has implicitly or explicitly refused to remedy the lack of conformity".[45] In our view, the concept of implicit refusal is not a sufficiently clear test to cover all the circumstances which would justify proceeding to a second tier remedy. We think it would be helpful to specify two other circumstances in which a consumer may rescind the contract or ask for a reduction in price.

8.144 The first is where goods are perceived as dangerous. One example which emerged from our consumer discussions was where the brakes failed on a new car. The consumer who had survived this experience felt strongly that she did not want to drive that make or model of car again. Another example might be where an electrical item explodes. The consumer may not feel safe in having the product in the house. We think that, in these circumstances, the consumer should be entitled to bypass the remedies of repair or replacement and proceed straight to rescission.

---

[44] See below, paras 8.180 to 8.187 on damages.

[45] Proposal for a directive on consumer rights, art 26(4)(a).

8.145 Secondly, we think that the consumer should be allowed to proceed to second tier remedies where the retailer has behaved so unreasonably as to undermine the consumer's trust. In civil law terms, this would be characterised as a breach of good faith. There are several cases where traders have deliberately delayed answering correspondence or providing information,[46] or (as in *Ritchie*[47]) unreasonably refused to tell the buyer what was wrong with the product. The UK courts have taken the view that unreasonable behaviour of this type should allow the buyer to seek a refund, even outside the original period for the right to reject. Again, we think that the CSD should recognise that unreasonable behaviour of this type should of itself permit a consumer to rescind the contract without proceeding through first tier remedies.

8.146 **We provisionally propose that the CSD should be reformed to allow a consumer to proceed to a second tier remedy when a product has proved to be dangerous or where the retailer has behaved so unreasonably as to undermine trust between the parties.**

Rescission and "deduction for use"

8.147 If a consumer progresses beyond the first tier remedies of the CSD, to the second tier remedy of rescission, they are entitled to a refund. In that case, the retailer is permitted to deduct an amount to reflect the consumer's use of the faulty goods. Section 48C(3) of SoGA states that:

> … if the buyer rescinds the contract, any reimbursement to the buyer may be reduced to take account of the use he has had of the goods since they were delivered.

8.148 This deduction for use concept is an option in the CSD[48] which the UK chose to implement, but many member states did not. Under the European Commission's proposals for a new directive, this option would be removed. Recital 41 of the proposed directive specifically states that "the consumer should not compensate the trader for the use of the defective goods".

Calculating the deduction for use

8.149 Currently, there is no indication as to how this reduction is to be calculated. In meetings, stakeholders complained that they were unsure how it should be calculated, and that it had the potential to lead to disputes.

---

[46] See, for example, *Clegg v Andersson T/A Nordic Marine* [2003] EWCA Civ 320; [2003] 1 All ER (Comm) 721 and *Bowes v Richardson & Son Limited*, 28 January 2004 (unreported). For discussion see Part 3.

[47] *J & H Ritchie Limited v Lloyd Limited* 2007 SC (HL) 89; [2007] 1 WLR 670; [2007] 2 All ER 353. It should be noted that this was not a consumer case.

[48] Recital 15.

8.150   There are several ways in which the deduction could be measured. One method is by reference to the second-hand value of goods; another by reference to the expected life-span of the goods, allowing straight-line depreciation. Willett and others have argued that the correct measure depends on how long the goods should have lasted – if, for example, the washing machine had an expected life-span of five years and broke down after a year, the deduction should typically be 20% of the price.[49] The consumer's loss is four years' loss of the washing machine, not the second-hand value after one year; he or she never intended to sell the machine at that point. We think that this is the best method of calculation.

8.151   The problem is that it is often difficult to estimate how long particular goods should be expected to last. It would be possible to draw up guidelines in collaboration with industry, similar to the "Retra Code",[50] showing how long a consumer durable can reasonably be expected to last. It would, however, be a considerable task to draw up guidelines for every category of consumer durable.

Consumers' views

8.152   The consumer research we commissioned showed that this concept was very unpopular with consumers. In fact, it was a rather inflammatory subject. Consumers felt that if they had been unfortunate enough to find themselves with a faulty product, and repairs and/or replacements had been unsuccessful, they would feel aggrieved if they were then charged for use of the product. They suggested that no reputable retailers would attempt to make a deduction for use.

8.153   Common sense tells us that in order to get to the second tier remedies, the consumer would probably have experienced considerable delay and inconvenience, and probably more than one attempt at repair or replacement. An additional question is whether, in the event that the retailer makes a deduction for use, the consumer can set off damages for the delay, inconvenience and other financial loss. Consumers felt that if the trader was going to reduce the refund to take account of the use of the (defective) goods, then they should be entitled to ask for compensation for time off work, telephone calls and alternative provision. The consumer could sue for damages, so a set off of this type is theoretically possible.

The overlap with domestic remedies

8.154   The deduction for use raises a further problem about how the CSD remedy of rescission overlaps with the right to reject. As we saw in Part 3, the right to reject may be suspended while the consumer seeks information about the product or asks for repairs.[51] This leads to questions about whether, after a failed repair, the consumer may short-circuit the CSD remedies by reviving their right to reject.

---

[49]   C Willett, M Morgan-Taylor and A Naidoo, "The Sale and Supply of Goods to Consumers Regulations" [2004] *Journal of Business Law* 94 at 114 to 115.

[50]   Retra is the Radio, Electrical and Television Retailers' Association; the code of practice is available at http://www.retra.co.uk/code.asp?p=13. For cars, HM Revenue and Customs also provide guidelines for depreciation.

[51]   See for example, *Clegg v Andersson T/A Nordic Marine* [2003] EWCA Civ 320; [2003] 1 All ER (Comm) 721 and *J & H Ritchie Limited v Lloyd Limited* 2007 SC (HL) 89; [2007] 1 WLR 670; [2007] 2 All ER 353.

8.155 The main practical difference between returning to the right to reject or proceeding to rescission is whether the consumer must give an allowance for use. Well informed consumers might be able to argue that they should not give such an allowance by invoking the principles set out in cases such as *Clegg*[52] and *Ritchie*.[53] Retailers in particular were keen that we should iron out this quirk in the law.

Conclusion

8.156 We think that the European Commission is right to remove the possibility of a "deduction for use". It is unpopular with consumers, uncertain and seldom used.[54] It also adds complications to the law, as consumers retaliate with damages claims, or attempt to circumvent it by claiming a revival of their right to reject.

8.157 **We ask consultees whether they agree that the "deduction for use" in the event of rescission should be abolished.**

Should the six-month reverse burden begin again after repair or replacement?

8.158 Section 48A (3) of SoGA states that:

> … goods which do not conform to the contract of sale at any time within the period of six months starting with the date on which the goods were delivered to the buyer must be taken not to have so conformed at that date.

8.159 Normally, the relevant "delivery" would be the point at which goods are first delivered to the consumer. The question that arises, however, is whether the redelivery of repaired goods, or the delivery of replacement goods, acts to restart the six-month reverse burden of proof. In other words, does a redelivery qualify as a relevant delivery?

8.160 In SoGA, delivery is defined as "voluntary transfer of possession from one person to another",[55] which could cover the situation of a redelivery. Elsewhere, in Part 5A of SoGA, however, the term is used in a manner which seems inconsistent with this reading. It states that a buyer has to give value for the use of the goods since "delivery".[56] If the consumer only had to give value for goods since their *re*delivery, a consumer would not be accounting for the benefit of goods prior to their repair.

---

[52] *Clegg v Andersson T/A Nordic Marine* [2003] EWCA Civ 320; [2003] 1 All ER (Comm) 721.

[53] *J & H Ritchie Limited v Lloyd Limited* 2007 SC (HL) 89; [2007] 1 WLR 670; [2007] 2 All ER 353. For discussion of this point, see paras 3.33 to 3.52.

[54] We have heard, however, about one large motor retailer which does make a deduction for both use and (straight-line) depreciation. In doing so it makes use of the guidelines published by HM Revenue and Customs.

[55] SoGA, s 61(1).

[56] SoGA, s 48C(3), quoted at para 8.147 above.

8.161 *Benjamin's Sale of Goods* argues in favour of restarting the six-month period upon redelivery. This is said to be "consistent with the thrust" of the European approach, though it is recognised that difficult problems may arise if different defects manifest themselves at different times.[57]

8.162 The retailer is obliged to provide goods which conform with the contract whenever they repair or replace goods. Our view is that the same logic which provides a six-month reverse burden of proof for the original delivery should also apply where there is a redelivery following cure.

8.163 **We provisionally propose that the six-month reverse burden of proof should recommence after goods are redelivered following repair or replacement.**

The proposed two-year cut-off

8.164 The CSD currently states that member states must allow consumers at least two years to bring a claim before the courts.[58] The UK exceeds this minimum. Instead, the limits which apply are those set in general contract law. In England there is a limitation period of six years and, in Scotland, a period of prescription of five years.

8.165 However, under the European Commission's proposed new directive, consumers would not be entitled to pursue a retailer for any fault which becomes apparent more than two years after delivery.[59]

8.166 In most circumstances, this is unlikely to cause a problem. For the great majority of consumer goods, any defect will become apparent quickly (within weeks or months, rather than years). For food, clothing, electronics or most household goods, it is difficult to imagine that faults will arise after two years.

8.167 Our concern, however, is that the provision may not be suitable for some unusual goods, which are intended to be long-lasting and where defects may take time to come to light. The most obvious example would be for building materials, where (for example) a steel joist collapses after 26 months, or water pipes crack in the first hard frost, two and a half years after they are installed. The provision would also apply where a consumer buys a valuable antique (such as a Fabergé egg) only to discover after a few years that it is not as described, and is in fact a fake.

---

[57] *Benjamin's Sale of Goods* (7th ed 2006) para 12-087. R Bradgate and C Twigg-Flesner, *Blackstone's Guide to Consumer Sales and Associated Guarantees* (2003) p 97 agrees that it would be "common sense" to restart the period, but says that this may go against a strict reading of the Directive.

[58] Art 5(1).

[59] Art 28(1).

8.168   It seems odd that a business in these circumstances would have a remedy, but an individual would not have a remedy. The justification for the two-year period is that it brings certainty to retailers, enabling them to close their books after two years. However, the retailer will not necessarily know whether the buyer was a consumer or a business. Business buyers will continue to be able to pursue claims within the limitation or prescriptive period.[60]

8.169   Our provisional view is that in most cases, a two-year cut-off is not needed, and that in some unusual cases it has the potential to cause problems. We would welcome views on this.

8.170   **We provisionally propose that the time limits for bringing a claim should continue to be those applying to general contractual claims within England, Wales and Scotland.**

8.171   **We welcome views on whether there is a need to prevent consumers from pursuing remedies where faults come to light more than two years after delivery. We also welcome views on whether this might cause problems in particular cases.**

WRONG QUANTITY

8.172   In Part 2 we describe the remedies currently available to consumers where the retailer delivers the wrong quantity under section 30 of SoGA. In consumer sales, this section is not compatible with the proposal for a new directive. At present, buyers have a choice between rejecting the goods or asking for a cure. Under the European Commission's proposals, the immediate right to reject would be lost. Where sales were conducted through a shop (rather than by distance methods or at the consumer's home) the consumer would need to give the retailer the opportunity to cure the defect.

8.173   In Part 2 we describe the duty to deliver the correct quantity of goods as an application of the more general duty to provide goods which correspond to their description. We would be interested to know whether there are any reasons to retain section 30 of SoGA as a distinct remedy for consumers, or whether the issue can simply be dealt with through the more general rules applying to non-conforming goods. Under our provisional proposals outlined above,[61] this would give consumers the right to reject within a normal period of 30 days.

8.174   **We welcome views on whether there are reasons to retain section 30 of SoGA for consumer sales, or whether cases where the wrong quantity is delivered can be dealt with through the application of general principles.**

LATE DELIVERY

8.175   In Part 2 we describe the remedies available when a delivery is late. The current law allows the consumer an automatic refund of their purchase price only where the delivery date is of the essence of the contract.

---

[60] In Scotland, the current law allows claims to be brought within five years from the date when the loss was, or could with reasonable diligence have been, discovered.

[61] See above, paras 8.42 to 8.77.

8.176 The European Commission has proposed increased protection in this area. The proposal for a new directive on consumer rights states that goods must be delivered within 30 days "unless the parties have agreed otherwise".[62] Where "the trader has failed to fulfil his obligation to deliver" the consumer is entitled to a full refund within seven days. This suggests that where the parties have agreed a delivery date, any failure to meet the delivery date would trigger a full refund.

8.177 The issue is of no practical consequence in distance selling (where the consumer has cancellation rights in any event). However, it appears to increase rights where the consumer chooses an item in a shop and the shop agrees (for example) "to deliver it on Tuesday". If the trader delivers on Wednesday, under current law, the consumer would only be entitled to a full refund it they made it clear that a Tuesday delivery was important to them.

8.178 We would welcome views on whether consumers should be entitled to a full refund for any failure to meet an agreed delivery date - or only where the delivery is particularly late or the consumer has made clear that the date is important to them.

8.179 **We seek consultees' views on whether consumers should be entitled to a full refund whenever the trader fails to meet an agreed delivery date. The alternative would be to retain the current law**.

DAMAGES

8.180 Stakeholders have universally agreed that it is essential to retain the domestic remedy of damages. One retailer pointed out that an important benefit of that remedy is that it requires consumers to mitigate their loss.

8.181 In the context of the CSD regime, there is some similarity between damages (the traditional domestic remedy) and price reduction (the CSD remedy). They will normally be calculated on the same basis: the difference between the value of the actual goods received and the value of the goods to which the consumer was entitled.[63] Crucially, though, damages can go further where consequences flow from the contract breach if such consequences were within the contemplation of the parties. Where, for example, a domestic appliance catches fire and the fire damages the consumer's house or furniture, there is obvious consequential loss.

8.182 The OFT Report on Consumer Detriment found that it is not uncommon in the UK for consumers to pay to have goods repaired at their own expense: it was found to occur in 15% of cases where the consumer had experienced a financial loss. There may be good reasons for the consumer to arrange a repair, for example, where a car develops a fault abroad, or where the consumer has lost confidence in the seller.

---

[62] Art 22(1).

[63] G Howells and S Weatherill, *Consumer Protection Law* (2nd ed 2005) p 201.

8.183   We have raised the question about whether a consumer can set off damages against an allowance for use following rescission.[64] This question leads to a more general discussion about the damages payable in a typical consumer case, where other financial loss has flowed from the purchase of faulty goods. Generally, claimants can claim for losses that are within contracting parties' reasonable contemplation as a not unlikely result of the breach of contract. The principles are set out in case law.[65] However, stakeholder feedback indicates that, in practice, consumers do not routinely obtain financial compensation even where they have suffered relevant financial loss.

8.184   The FDS research also shows that in some cases consumers may feel that they should be compensated for distress and inconvenience caused by faulty goods and/or the repair and replacement process. Generally speaking, damages are not recoverable under these heads in English law. However, where part of the object of a contract is to provide pleasure, relaxation or peace of mind, damages for disappointment can be awarded.[66] Scots law provides for damages to be payable for trouble and inconvenience resulting from a breach of contract, and, in certain circumstances, for "mental distress" or "hurt feelings" arising from such a breach.[67]

8.185   These types of cases are seldom litigated and even more rarely reported. We therefore seek views on whether further guidance is needed on the circumstances in which damages should be payable.

8.186   **We provisionally propose that the right to damages should be retained in UK law.**

8.187   **We seek views on whether the issue of damages should be left to the common law or whether guidance would be helpful on the circumstances in which damages should be payable to consumers. In particular, should damages be available for loss of earnings, distress, disappointment, loss of amenity and inconvenience? If so, for which types of goods, and in which circumstances?**

---

[64]   See above, para 7.39.

[65]   *Hadley v Baxendale* (1854) 9 Exch 341; *Victoria Laundry (Windsor) Ltd v Newman Industries Ltd* [1949] 2 KB 528; and *The Heron II* [1969] 1 AC 350.

[66]   *Farley v Skinner* [2001] UKHL 49; [2002] 2 AC 732.

[67]   See above, para 7.45.

INTEGRATION OF CSD REMEDIES WITH THE RIGHT TO REJECT

Rejection with three possible options

8.188   In Part 2 we explain that the *rejection* of goods and the *termination* of the sales contract are two separate concepts. We use the short-hand term of the "right to reject" to mean rejection and termination (including a refund) or, in Scots law, the consumer treating the contract as repudiated by the trader.[68] There are circumstances where the rejection of goods (that is, the refusal to accept goods) will not be followed by termination of the contract. For example, the consumer may reject goods and give the trader an opportunity to cure the fault.

8.189   We have been considering how the right to reject (under SoGA) might be better integrated with the CSD remedies in order to make the remedies regime simpler. This could be done by combining the right to reject with repair and replacement. The three first instance remedies could be joined under the umbrella of the concept of rejection.

8.190   A new Sale of Goods Act could provide that a consumer buyer of faulty goods can *reject* them with three possible remedies of first instance as follows:

> (1) **Termination plus full refund** if within a normal period of 30 days - this is what we currently call the right to reject.
>
> (2) & (3) Alternatively, a consumer can request either **repair** or **replacement**.[69]

8.191   If the retailer cannot carry out either repair or replacement without significant inconvenience to the consumer or within a reasonable time, the consumer can opt for the second tier remedies of termination ("rescission") or a reduction in price.[70] Second tier termination could be seen as a revival of the first tier right to terminate, which comes into play where repair or replacement are not successfully undertaken.

8.192   A diagram of the remedial regime would look like this, stressing the three remedies that consumers most use: refund, repair and replacement.

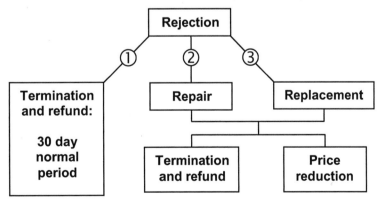

<hr>

[68]   That is, rescinding the contract as a result of material breach.

[69]   In accordance with the CSD, the retailer could decline that request and offer the alternative first tier remedy if the request is impossible or disproportionate when compared with the other first tier remedy.

[70]   This is also in accordance with the CSD provisions.

8.193 **We provisionally propose that SoGA and the CSD remedies should be better integrated in a single instrument, by use of the concept of *rejection*.**

A right to reject after repairs have failed?

8.194 As we have seen, if a consumer seeks to exercise the right to reject but is persuaded by the retailer to allow one or more attempts at repair, then under current law, the right to reject is effectively suspended. The consumer may exercise the right to reject if the repair(s) fail.

8.195 In the context of the current law, some retailers raised the point that, if repairs fail, there is confusion as to whether the consumer is pursuing a revived right to reject, or rescission under the CSD. They asked us to clarify this issue.

8.196 Under current law, it would appear that a consumer who asks for a repair quickly (within a few weeks) would have different rights from a consumer who buys a good with a latent defect which does not become visible for a couple of months. The first may ask for refund more readily (without showing unreasonable delay or significant inconvenience) and does not have to give an allowance for use.

8.197 In the past, the Law Commissions believed that the continuation of the right to reject during a period of repair was a necessary safeguard for the consumer.[71] Previously, some retailers would attempt to bypass the right to reject by persuading consumers to accept attempts at repair. Sometimes, retailers' attempts at repairs were not genuine, and this was simply a ploy. Consumers were left with faulty goods on their hands when they had tried to co-operate with retailers, which was thought to be unfair. In the 1987 Report, the Law Commissions were keen to encourage attempts at "cure" without penalising the consumer, or prejudicing the consumer's right to reject.

8.198 It still seems undesirable that a consumer who expresses a desire to exercise the right to reject but is persuaded by a retailer to allow an attempt at repair thereby reduces his or her rights. This is especially true if the consumer is merely trying to accommodate the retailer.

8.199 Nevertheless, the existence of two separate regimes adds to complexity. When, several months down the line, the consumer is arguing about whether to accept a second repair, it would seem odd that the consumer's rights would depend on the exact date on which he or she requested the first repair. We think that a dual regime of this sort would be too difficult for consumers to understand.

8.200 In the interests of simplification, we think that where a consumer has agreed to a repair, the separate right to reject should cease. Instead, the matter should be dealt with in the way that we have outlined above in discussing possible reforms of the CSD.[72] In other words, the right to a refund should depend on the number of repairs or replacements, whether there has been unreasonable delay or significant inconvenience, and whether the product was dangerous or the retailer behaved unreasonably.

---

[71] See s 35(6)(a) of SoGA which makes this explicit, and paras 5.26-5.29 of the 1987 Report.

[72] See above, paras 8.135, 8.136, 8.141, 8.146 and 8.157.

8.201 In saying this, we think it important that second tier rights should be made accessible and consumers should not have to argue about an appropriate allowance for the short use they have had from the product. If agreeing to a repair shortly after purchase meant that consumers were forced into the current CSD regime, we think that consumer rights would be significantly reduced. Consumers would have all the difficulties of arguing over how many repairs should be attempted, and would not be protected should the product prove dangerous or the retailer uncooperative.

8.202 **We provisionally propose that once a consumer has accepted a repair, their right to reject ceases. If the repair fails, the consumer should proceed to a second tier remedy along the lines we have proposed in relation to the reform of the CSD.**

CONSUMER EDUCATION

8.203 Stakeholders emphasised the need for consumer education about the legal remedies available for faulty goods. Whilst everyone appears to agree that education regarding consumer legal rights would be highly beneficial, the more difficult question is how this should be done. There has been no consensus in our discussions with stakeholders. Willett and others have suggested:

> First of all, it is important that as much as possible is done to make the new regime work in practice. Vital to this is seeking to make consumers as aware as possible of their rights. There seems to be a strong case for requiring a standard form summary at the point of sale of the basic package of rights and remedies discussed above. This would need to do no more than indicate that if goods are defective, there *may* be a legal right to repair/replacement, price reduction or some form of refund. It might also be desirable to develop sector-specific codes of practice which can provide detailed consumer focused guidance on the various new concepts emanating from the Directive, eg when a repair or replacement is "impossible" or "disproportionate", and how reductions in refunds based on beneficial use should be calculated.[73]

"This does not affect your statutory rights"

8.204 Our research highlighted particular problems with the phrase *"this does not affect your statutory rights"*. Consumers are familiar with this phrase as it appears on the back of many shop receipts and on signs about shops' returns policies. Despite this familiarity, however, it is clear that few understand what the phrase means; still fewer understand what their statutory rights actually are.[74]

---

[73] "The Sale and Supply of Goods to Consumers Regulations" [2004] *Journal of Business Law* 94 at 118.

[74] See Appendix A.

8.205   Since 1978, it has been obligatory for traders to notify consumers that their statutory rights are not affected by statements relating to the traders' obligations.[75] The "statutory rights" concerned include certain sections of the Sale of Goods Act 1979 and the Supply of Goods and Services Act 1982.

8.206   The 1976 Order that created the obligation ceased to have effect when the Unfair Commercial Practices Directive (UCPD)[76] was implemented into UK law by the Consumer Protection from Unfair Trading Regulations 2008.[77] The new Regulations did, however, insert essentially the same obligation into other legislation.[78]

8.207   Article 6(2) of the CSD has a separate requirement regarding notices. It requires a statement that the consumer "has legal rights under applicable national legislation" and that they are not affected by the trader's guarantee.

8.208   The phrase "this does not affect your statutory rights" was taken from the wording of the 1976 Order, which provided that there must be a statement:

> … to the effect that the first mentioned statement does not or will not affect the statutory rights of a consumer.[79]

Whilst the popular phrase was not specifically mandated by the 1976 Order, it was very much in line with the language that was used. It is likely that the "statutory rights" phrasing also satisfies the current Regulations, which are couched in similar terms.[80]

8.209   However, the phrase "this does not affect your statutory rights" has been criticised under the Unfair Terms in Consumer Contracts Regulations 1999 (UTCCRs). The Office of Communications (Ofcom) has considered two complaints against firms' contracts on the grounds that the phrase is not in plain and intelligible language.

8.210   In a complaint against UK Online Limited,[81] Ofcom considered a contractual term which stated:

> These terms and conditions do not affect your statutory rights.

---

[75]   Consumer Transactions (Restrictions on Statements) Order 1976 SI 1976 No 1813.

[76]   Directive 2005/29/EC.

[77]   SI 2008 No 1277. Sch 2, para 69 of the Regulations repealed the Enterprise Act 2002, s 10(2), which had previously saved the Fair Trading Act 1973, s 22. The 1976 Order was made under that section.

[78]   Sch 2, para 97 inserted a new Reg 15(2A) into the Sale and Supply of Goods to Consumers Regulations 2002 SI 2002 No 3045. It reads:
   "(2A) The guarantor shall also ensure that the guarantee contains a statement that the consumer has statutory rights in relation to the goods which are sold or supplied and that those rights are not affected by the guarantee."

[79]   Consumer Transactions (Restrictions on Statements) Order 1976 SI 1976 No 1813, Art 4(ii).

[80]   Sale and Supply of Goods to Consumers Regulations 2002, Reg 15(2A) (see above).

[81]   Case reference CW/00887/01/06, available at:
   http://www.ofcom.org.uk/bulletins/comp_bull_index/comp_bull_ccases/closed_all/cw_887/.

Ofcom's conclusion was that "the use of legal jargon such as 'statutory rights' did not express the term in plain and intelligible language".[82] UK Online agreed to change the term to:

> These terms and conditions do not affect your rights under law. If you require any advice or assistance we would suggest you contact your local branch of the citizens' advice bureau who should be able to help.

8.211 In another Ofcom complaint, this time against Hutchison 3G Limited ("3 Mobile"),[83] the original terms referred to provisions of the Consumer Protection (Distance Selling) Regulations 2000. This was criticised:

> Ofcom regarded the reference to statutory provisions to potentially breach Regulation 7 [of the UTCCR], which states that contracts should be expressed in plain, intelligible language.

8.212 The resulting term removed the reference to specific statutes, but remained in terms of "statutory rights":

> … if you are a consumer, any statutory rights which you may have, which cannot be excluded or limited, will not be affected by this section. For more information contact your local authority Trading Standards Department or Citizens Advice Bureau.

8.213 The case also resulted in a change from "your statutory rights are not affected" to:

> If you are a consumer, the terms of this agreement will not affect any of your statutory rights which you have, which cannot be excluded by this agreement. For more information on your statutory rights, contact your local authority Trading Standards Department or Citizens Advice Bureau.

8.214 We have considered how the phrase: *"This does not affect your statutory rights"* might be simplified, as wording of that nature remains a requirement under the CSD and UCPD. Of the various possible approaches, we favour:

> This does not reduce your legal rights.
>
> For further information about your legal rights please contact [name and contact details of Consumer Direct or other appropriate source of information].

Not only would this wording clarify what is meant, but it would also provide a means for consumers to find out about their legal rights. However, if a specific organisation were to be named, it would have resource implications, which we discuss in paragraph 9.67.

---

[82] As required by the Unfair Terms in Consumer Contracts Regulations 1999 SI 1999 No 2083, Reg 7(1).

[83] Case reference CW/00888/01/06, available at: http://www.ofcom.org.uk/bulletins/comp_bull_index/comp_bull_ccases/closed_all/cw_888/.

8.215 Another possibility would be to provide a summary of the consumer's legal remedies for faulty goods which could be publicised at point of sale. It is possible that this could be in the form of leaflets or signage.

8.216 **We ask consultees to comment upon how the aim of increasing awareness of consumer legal rights for faulty goods might be achieved.**

8.217 **In particular, should there be a summary of consumer legal rights for faulty goods available at point of sale? If so, which form should it take?**

8.218 **We ask consultees whether they agree that notices displayed in shops should:**

(1) **use the expression "This does not reduce your legal rights" rather than "This does not affect your statutory rights".**

(2) **say how a consumer could obtain further information about their legal rights.**

PART 9
ASSESSING THE IMPACT OF REFORM

9.1 In this Part, we discuss the social and economic impact of our provisional proposals. We start by summarising the problem and our policy objectives, and outline the different options we have considered. We then set out the main costs and benefits associated with each option, before referring to the available evidence.

THE PROBLEM

9.2 The current law states that goods must meet certain standards. For example, goods must be of satisfactory quality, fit for purpose and correspond with their description.[1] These standards are reasonably clear and well understood.

9.3 The problem lies in the remedies available to consumers when goods fail to meet these standards. The law in this area is overly complex and uncertain; shop managers find it too difficult to understand or to communicate to sales staff. Similarly, consumer advisers often struggle with its intricacies, and feel uncertain about communicating it to consumers. This causes unnecessary disputes.

POLICY OBJECTIVE AND INTENDED EFFECTS

9.4 Our aim is to simplify the remedies available to consumers when they buy faulty goods. We wish to bring the law into line with accepted good practice and provide appropriate remedies which allow consumers to participate with confidence in the market place.

9.5 The intended benefits are a simpler legal system, leading to reduced training costs, fewer disputes and increased consumer confidence.

WHAT POLICY OPTIONS HAVE BEEN CONSIDERED?

9.6 The central issue is the question of when consumers should be entitled to return faulty goods and receive a refund, rather than being required to accept a repair or replacement. As we have seen, under current law consumers have "a right to reject" goods and receive a refund, provided that they exercise it within "a reasonable time". It is very difficult to say what a reasonable time is, though in many cases we think it may be around a month.

9.7 We identified four possible approaches to the right to reject:

   (1)   *Do nothing*. This would leave the law as it is, with all its existing complexities. These are described at length in Part 7.

---

[1]   See Sale of Goods Act 1979, ss 13 and 14. Where goods are sold by sample, the whole must also correspond with the sample (s 15).

(2) *Abolition.* UK law would no longer recognise a right to reject. Where goods developed a fault the consumer's primary remedy would be to ask for a repair or replacement. Consumers would be entitled to a refund only if the repair or replacement proved impossible or disproportionate, or took too long or caused significant inconvenience.

(3) *Extension.* Under this option, consumers could return the goods and receive a refund even for latent defects which became apparent months (or possibly years) after purchase.

(4) *Retention with clarification.* The right to reject would be retained as a short-term remedy, but legislation would clarify how long it should last, together with related simplifications.

A SUMMARY OF COSTS AND BENEFITS

9.8 Below we summarise our provisional conclusions on the main costs and benefits of each of the four options we have considered. In the next section, we set out the evidence for these provisional conclusions.

Do nothing

9.9 The main problem with the "do nothing" option is that it imposes an administrative burden on retailers, leading to increased staff training, unnecessary disputes and legal costs.

9.10 The Davidson Review identified the problems. It commented that the law on consumer remedies is too complex: "it is not easy for consumers to understand what their rights are and this leads to dissatisfied customers and increased amounts of litigation".[2] This can be a burden on business, as retailers struggle to train staff. The cost of litigation might also be significant. The Davidson Review received evidence that some of the large retail chains had teams dealing with disputes over faulty goods on a full-time basis. Consumer groups also find it difficult to give clear advice.

Abolishing the right to reject

9.11 Abolishing the right to reject might reduce costs to businesses, but our consumer research suggests that it would undermine consumer confidence.

9.12 In many cases, consumers are happy to accept repairs or replacements. However, they value the right to return goods if an early fault suggests that the goods suffer from design faults or generally poor workmanship. Consumers are particularly worried about becoming locked into a cycle of failed repairs. Our research suggested that abolition would reduce consumers' confidence in buying non-branded goods from unknown retailers because they could not be sure that they would get their money back in the event of problems arising.

9.13 Abolition might also increase costs to consumers and add to the number of disputes (over, for example, what amounts to "significant inconvenience").

---

[2] Davidson Review, *Final Report* (November 2006) para 3.11.

Extending the right to reject to cover latent defects

9.14 We considered whether consumers should be entitled to return goods and obtain a refund when something went wrong long after purchase. Extension would reduce costs to consumers and might increase consumer confidence.

9.15 It would, however, increase direct costs to businesses. In some cases, goods would be returned where it was more economical to repair them. Goods with the potential to be repaired might have to be disposed of, leading to a possible negative impact on the environment produced by increased electrical waste and landfill.

9.16 Furthermore, we thought that the remedy could be abused, with consumers deliberately breaking goods because they had no further use for them. A long right to reject might also make it more difficult for small retailers to pass problems back to manufacturers or to close their books.

Retention with clarification

9.17 Stakeholders told us that retaining a short-term right to reject provided an acceptable balance between maintaining consumer confidence and preventing unnecessary waste.

9.18 Our provisional proposals are aimed at retaining the broad outline of the existing law, but simplifying and clarifying the way in which the law operates. We propose a balanced package of measures which will maintain consumer protection at existing levels, reduce the administrative burden on businesses, and reduce unnecessary disputes.

9.19 Some of our individual proposals would increase protection while others would decrease it. The measures designed to increase protection are:

(1) The six-month reverse burden of proof will apply to the traditional UK remedies;

(2) Legislation will clarify that the six-month period restarts when repaired or replaced goods are redelivered;

(3) Consumers may rescind the contract where goods are dangerous or retailers have damaged trust through their unreasonable behaviour;

(4) The abolition of the deduction for use when a contract is rescinded.

9.20 Conversely, the measures which would decrease protection are:

(1) In Part 8 we discuss whether a shorter period of time to reject goods in work and materials contracts and contracts for exchange;

(2) We also propose a clarification that the right to reject does not revive after a failed repair. Instead the consumer would move to a second tier remedy, such as rescission.

9.21 Many of these measures clarify and simplify the law, but have only minor practical effects. For example, in practice, as a matter of common sense, durable goods which break within 30 days are presumed to be faulty at purchase. In theory, the abolition of the deduction for use would disadvantage retailers, but our research suggested that it is rarely applied.

9.22 Some provisions may also represent current law. For example, it is likely that the courts would hold that the six-month period restarted after a redelivery.[3] Furthermore, under the current law, consumers could argue that they should receive a full refund where the retailer behaves unreasonably. However, consumers would have to use the complex arguments set out in the *Ritchie*[4] case, rather than the more straightforward ones which we propose.

9.23 The change would be greater if it decided that consumers should have less time to reject goods under non-sales contracts where, for example, they buy double-glazing or fitted kitchens. However, the extended right to reject in non-sales contracts is not well known,[5] and is extremely uncertain in its application. It is always open for a retailer to argue that the good was not sold as part of the work contract, but under a separate contract. Although some consumers may be disadvantaged by this change, it could be argued that the overall effect of our reforms will benefit consumers by providing them with greater clarity and certainty, thereby strengthening their bargaining position in the event of a dispute.

Conclusion

9.24 Our provisional conclusion is that abolishing the right to reject might lead to an unacceptable loss of consumer confidence. Extension, however, might add to waste and penalise small retailers who could not pass costs back to manufacturers. There is also a danger that unscrupulous consumers could abuse an extended right to reject, leading to price increases.

9.25 **We provisionally conclude that the balance of costs and benefits favours retaining the right to reject with appropriate clarification (in particular about how long it lasts).**

EVIDENCE BASE

9.26 In this section we discuss the effect of the law of consumer remedies on different aspects of the economy and environment. We start by looking at four general issues:

    (1)   the effects on consumer confidence;

    (2)   the costs and benefits to consumers;

    (3)   the costs and benefits to businesses;

---

[3] See above, para 7.66.

[4] *J & H Ritchie Limited v Lloyd Limited* 2007 SC (HL) 89; [2007] 1 WLR 670; [2007] 2 All ER 353.

[5] See *Jones v Gallagher (trading as Gallery Kitchens and Bathrooms)* [2004] EWCA Civ 10; [2005] 1 Lloyd's Reports 377, discussed above at paras 3.44 to 3.46.

(4)   the administrative burden on businesses.

We then consider the impact of the proposals on competition; on small firms; on the environment and on publicly funded advice services.

Consumer confidence

9.27   Consumer spending is a major part of the UK economy. Though it is not easy to reconcile all the statistics, it is likely that consumer spending represents approximately 60% of the UK's gross domestic product.[6] UK consumer spending[7] has grown strongly over the past few years, increasing from approximately £600 billion in 2000[8] to nearly £840 billion in 2007.[9] Of that, we estimate just under half is spent on goods.[10] That figure translates to around £400 billion per annum. In comparison to other EU member states, the UK's consumer expenditure is above average. Two reports from the European statistics source "Eurostat" show that UK consumers spend more than the average European.[11]

9.28   In the 2008 OFT report on consumer detriment, a third of respondents reported one or more problems with goods or services, amounting to an estimated 26.5 million problems over a 12 month period. Of these, we estimate that at least 10 million related to faulty goods. Although most disputes about faulty goods are minor (involving less than £100), collectively the impact may be significant.

9.29   Research shows that when consumers are confident of their rights, they are prepared to spend more. In Akerlof's seminal paper relating to the used car market, he demonstrates that the existence of "lemons" undermines consumer confidence to such an extent that the market for used cars may be almost destroyed.[12] Commercial guarantees can go some way to upholding confidence, but legal guarantees can go further. Minimum levels of quality, aligned with remedies, can ensure that consumers trust the marketplace.

9.30   This concept has become government policy:

---

[6]   According to Eurostat, *Europe in figures: Eurostat yearbook 2008* (2008) p 232, consumer spending in the UK was 61.9% of GDP in 2000 and 60.6% of GDP in 2005. However, Eurostat, *Economic portrait of the European Union 2002* (2003) p 25, states that in 2001 household consumption amounted to 66.3% of GDP.

[7]   That is "household spending", some of which does not fall within the scope of our project.

[8]   Office for National Statistics, *United Kingdom National Accounts: The Blue Book 2007* (2007) p 200.

[9]   Office for National Statistics, *Consumer Trends: Quarter 4 2007* (2008) p 16.

[10]   In 2007 consumer spending represented nearly £840 billion, of which approximately £406 billion was accounted for by: food, drink and tobacco; other "non-durable" goods; "semi-durable" goods; and "durable" goods. These figures are taken from Office for National Statistics, *Consumer Trends: Quarter 4 2007* (2008).

[11]   Eurostat, *Economic portrait of the European Union 2002* (2003) and Eurostat, *Europe in figures: Eurostat yearbook 2008* (2008).

[12]   G A Akerlof, "The Market for 'Lemons': Quality Uncertainty and the Market Mechanism" (1970) 84 *The Quarterly Journal of Economics* 488.

The Government is committed to ensuring consumers get a fair deal, value for money, safe and high quality products, and greater choice. This is not only good for consumers, it is also good for British business.

Business needs demanding, confident consumers who encourage higher standards and innovation. It needs effective enforcement of consumer standards, to drive out the rogues who compete unfairly.[13]

9.31 The Government has been committed to the goal of increasing consumer confidence for many years. The Government published a White Paper in July 1999 entitled "Modern Markets: Confident Consumers", which describes the circular relationship between well-informed, confident consumers, and strong competitive businesses. The Paper explains that knowledgeable, demanding consumers drive standards upwards; they encourage innovation and vigorous competition between firms on an equal basis; and firms compete in order to attract and maintain custom. In 2005, the Government reiterated its view that empowering consumers drives competition and is central to its strategy for improving the UK's consumer regime.[14]

9.32 It was clear from the FDS research that retailers' returns policies affected consumers' decisions on where to shop. Consumers said that they would deliberately choose a store which is known to have a particularly good returns policy. This made them more confident about spending money in the store. Finding out about a store's returns policy, however, had a transactional cost; there was a limit to the amount of time and effort consumers were prepared to put into finding out about the policies of individual retailers. The result was that consumers were far better informed about the returns policy of major retailers (such as Marks and Spencer and John Lewis) than about those of small or medium enterprises.

9.33 The FDS research indicates that the right to reject, in particular, gives consumers the confidence to purchase brands and goods which are unfamiliar to them, and from retailers whose policies they do not know. It allows consumers to be more adventurous, by selecting unknown (and cheaper) brands. This is because they know that if the goods do not work when they get them home, they can return them and get their money back. They do not have to take the risk of shoddy workmanship or design faults which will reappear in repaired or replacement products. Nor do they have to take the time and trouble to enquire into the shop's policy before parting with their money.

9.34 It would appear that valued and familiar consumer rights (including a right to reject) encourage innovative and competitive markets because consumers make purchases which they might not otherwise make.

---

[13] Taken from the BERR website: http://www.berr.gov.uk/consumers/policy/index.html. This same belief has been noted in the European context: see the Sutherland Report (*The Internal Market after 1992: Meeting the Challenge* SEC (92) 2044 (1992)).

[14] Department of Trade and Industry, "*A Fair Deal For All. Extending Competitive Markets: Empowered Consumers, Successful Business*" (2005).

Costs and benefits to consumers

9.35 The recent OFT report found that the overall level of consumer detriment due to faulty goods and services amounts to £6.6 billion per year.[15] A disproportionate amount of this detriment was generated by problems with insurance, but the evidence also demonstrates that issues relevant to our project can cost customers hundreds of pounds per problem.[16]

9.36 Many disputes are resolved in accordance with the law, but the research indicates that a large number of disputes are not resolved completely.[17] In each of the cases where there is no resolution, the consumer is left to bear at least some of the burden. For example, 15% of people spend money putting things right at their own expense.[18] Consumers were particularly likely to experience consumer detriment when they bought personal computers, glazing and large domestic appliances.

9.37 Consumers also suffer from detriment in ways which are not calculated in financial terms. As we discussed in Part 5, much personal time is spent resolving issues[19] which can leave the consumer feeling frustrated and angry.[20] The most vulnerable consumers, in the lowest social grades, experience greater effects both in terms of stress and their ability to spend on other items.[21]

9.38 Consumers benefit from strong, clear consumer rights, but would bear the cost if the effects were passed on in higher prices.

Costs and benefits to businesses

9.39 There is clearly a cost to retailers in receiving returned products and refunding the purchase price. The value of many goods drops sharply as soon as they are delivered. The retailer not only loses the profit from the sale but may also be left with goods worth less than their wholesale value. At worst, the retailer may have to bear the cost of disposing of a worthless product.

9.40 New cars are particularly prone to losing value on sale. The Retail Motor Industry Federation told us that new cars generally lose 20% to 30% of their value as soon as they are driven off the forecourt. Motor retailers said that they responded to the current law by carrying out careful checks on new cars before they sold them to prevent problems occurring on delivery (sometimes known as the "50 point check"). They also provided quick and efficient repairs and courtesy cars, to encourage consumers with a right to reject to agree to a repair. They were concerned, however, about any extension of the right to reject.

---

[15] Office of Fair Trading, *Consumer detriment: Assessing the frequency and impact of consumer problems with goods and services* (April 2008) para 4.4.

[16] Above, chart 4.5.

[17] Between 33% and 43% of disputes were not completely resolved (according to the consumer) in the categories relevant to this report: above, chart 6.2.

[18] Above, chart 4.12.

[19] Above, chart 5.1.

[20] Above, chart 5.3.

[21] Above, p 48.

9.41 Large retailers will seek to pass these costs back to manufacturers whereas smaller businesses may lack bargaining power. We explore this issue in greater detail below when looking at the position of small businesses. It would also be of significant concern if our proposals were to add to waste by causing products which could be repaired to be sent for disposal. Again, we consider this cost below, when looking at the environmental impact.

9.42 In Part 8, we expressed concern that an extended right to reject might be abused by some unscrupulous consumers. Consumers might claim that products were faulty when they were not, simply to recoup the purchase price. If this were to happen, the cost would be borne by all consumers in the form of increased prices.

9.43 Most businesses experience increased consumer protection as a cost. There is evidence, however, that effective dispute resolution increases sales. A survey by the OFT found that 70% of consumers who have had their complaint resolved satisfactorily will continue to trade with the same company.[22] The FDS research showed that consumers were influenced by a good returns policy in deciding where to shop.

The administrative burden on business

9.44 Although consumer protection is a vital plank to consumer confidence, it can impose a significant administrative burden on business. In all, the cost of government regulation has been estimated to be between £1.4 billion and £4.2 billion per year.[23] Administrative burdens created by consumer law alone have been estimated at around £1.25 billion a year, of which £770 million is taken up by external costs and overheads.[24] With such large figures, even comparably minor improvements can lead to significantly lower overheads for the business world.

9.45 Five factors have been identified as important in relation to administrative burdens:[25]

(1) *The volume and complexity of regulations.* Where the number of regulations is high, businesses have to turn to professional advisors to explain the business's obligations. Those advisors will also be used to explain regulations which are overly complex.

(2) *Regulatory change.* Where the regulatory framework is constantly in flux, businesses will not trust that they are up-to-date, and will turn to others to research and confirm the position.

---

[22] OFT Competition Act and Consumer Rights (May 2004).

[23] Better Regulation Executive, *Regulation and Business Advice* (2007) p 8. The higher figure was calculated on the basis of the Government's administrative burdens exercise, while the lower figure comes from a private sector consultancy.

[24] BERR, *Consumer Law Review: Call for Evidence* (May 2008) pp 8 and 9. These are based on the Better Regulation Executive's database of administrative burdens.

[25] Better Regulation Executive, *Regulation and Business Advice* (2007) p 9. The headings are repeated here, in a different order, and with different explanations.

(3) *Poor quality of government guidance.* Where guidance is scant, or unhelpful, there is considerable uncertainty for businesses. As stakeholders informed us, in respect of the guidance which they had seen, advice that fails to address the difficult issues is useless. Guidance should focus on business processes rather than legal structures.[26]

(4) *Uncertainty, risk and lack of confidence.* Government advice which is hedged around by disclaimers is of little use to businesses, who want to be able to rely on it. The Better Regulation Executive report admits that not all situations can be covered by guidance, but suggests that the disclaimer should be set out in a more positive way:

> Following this advice is not compulsory and you are free to take other action. But if you follow this guidance you will normally be doing enough to comply with the law.

(5) *Low awareness of government guidance.* Even where good advice is available, there is some evidence that businesses find it hard to access. The main Government portal for business advice is www.businesslink.gov.uk, but around only 6% of businesses are aware of it.[27]

9.46 It might be added that a proliferation of advice is unlikely to reduce administrative burdens. At best, it will require more time to read and compare. At worst, it could be contradictory and confuse matters further. The Better Regulation Executive report also stresses the need to consider guidance early on in the reform process, to ensure ease of use for businesses.

9.47 Businesses appear to agree with these criticisms of government advice as it stands. The stakeholders that we spoke to asked for more guidance, and 92% of those responding to the Hampton report in 2005 wanted more guidance from regulators.[28]

9.48 Thus, the type and content of guidance needs careful consideration. The rewards, however, are high. Better guidance which enables businesses to ensure self-compliance could save the economy significant amounts of money.

SPECIFIC IMPACT TESTS

9.49 We have considered the specific impact of our proposals in four areas of particular relevance. These are the impact on competition; on small firms; on the environment; and on publicly funded advice and assistance.

---

[26] Above, para 35.

[27] Quoted above, para 15.

[28] P Hampton for HM Treasury, *Reducing administrative burdens: effective inspection and enforcement* (March 2005) p 5.

Competition assessment

9.50 As described above, our research indicates that a basic floor of consumer rights makes consumers more prepared to buy unfamiliar or unadvertised products from unknown retailers. A base level of remedies provides a risk/reward ratio that allows new providers to enter the market at a competitive price.

9.51 On the other hand, if the law were to impose excessive consumer rights, this would increase prices. It would prevent consumers from exercising choices about the balance between price and quality which most met their needs. Consumers might be forced to buy a better quality of good than they wished at an excessive price.

9.52 It would appear that competition is best served by a balanced approach. The law should provide a floor of familiar and valued rights. We think that a clarified right to reject would give consumers confidence that the goods they buy will live up to what has been promised and meet their legitimate expectations. They will then know that if the goods are not as promised, they can get their money back. However, additional rights (such as an extended right to reject) would be best left to the market.

Impact on small firms

9.53 Small firms are an important part of the retail sector. In 2007 there were 317,450 businesses with fewer than 50 employees in the retail or repair business (dealing with products other than motor cars). They accounted for a quarter of all retail turnover.[29]

9.54 Ethnic minority businesses are concentrated within this sector.[30] Small shops are particularly likely to be Asian-owned. Some studies suggest that as many as three-quarters of all independently-owned single retail outlets are Asian.[31]

9.55 Small firms are especially sensitive to the effects we have outlined above. First, they may find it difficult to cope with the present complexity in the law, lacking the in-house legal resources of large retailers. Studies show, for example, that they are often over-represented as defendants in small claims proceedings, and find the litigation process particularly stressful.[32]

---

[29] See www.stats.berr.gov.uk/ed/sme.

[30] Of ethnic minority-led businesses with employees in the UK, 87% are in the service sector, compared with only 72% of non ethnic minority-led businesses. See www.berr.gov.uk/files/file38247.pdf.

[31] For further discussion, see "The contribution of Asian-owned businesses to London's economy" GLA Economics (June 2005) p 13, at http://www.london.gov.uk/mayor/economic_unit/docs/asian_businesses.pdf. Although this looks specifically at the importance of Asian-owned businesses within London, it also summarises research on the issue within the UK.

[32] J Baldwin, *Small Claims in the County Courts in England and Wales* (1997) pp 26 and 100.

9.56 Secondly, small firms would be the first to be affected by a change in consumer confidence. Without the right to reject, consumers would continue to buy from large firms with well-known reputations. They would, however, become more reluctant to shop from a small store whose returns policy was unknown. Any reduction in consumer rights is likely to be accompanied by considerable publicity. Major stores would be able to use their public relations departments to emphasise their own excellent policies on returns but this might be at the expense of smaller firms.

9.57 Thirdly, small firms would be disproportionately affected by an extension of consumer rights. This is because they would find it more difficult to pass the costs of faulty goods to the manufacturer. Where a manufacturer sells faulty goods to a retailer, the law implies terms that goods should correspond with their description or sample, and should be of satisfactory quality or fit for the buyer's purpose.[33] These are similar (though not identical) to those for consumers. However, a manufacturer may use its bargaining position to exclude its liability for breach of these terms, in so far as it is reasonable to do so.[34] We were told that manufacturers frequently impose time limits, stating (for example) that they will not recompense retailers for the cost of faulty products unless they are notified of the problem within three months of delivery to the retailer. However, the retailer may not be aware of the problem until the goods are bought, used by the consumer and then returned. If consumer rights were to be extended significantly, small businesses might be squeezed between the consumers and the manufacturer.

9.58 Our conclusion is that the greatest benefit to small firms lies in our preferred option, which is to retain the right to reject but to clarify it.

Impact on the environment

9.59 Any policy which encouraged goods to be disposed of rather than repaired would have an impact on the environment. The cost of disposal can be significant. From April 2008, the landfill tax has risen by £8 a tonne, and will do so each year for the next three years. By 2010/11, landfill tax will be £48 a tonne.[35]

---

[33] Sale of Goods Act 1979, ss 13 and 14.

[34] Unfair Contract Terms Act 1977, ss 6(3) and 7(3) in England and Wales, and ss 20(2)(ii) and 21(1)(a)(ii) in Scotland.

[35] http://www.defra.gov.uk/ENVIRONMENT/waste/topics/index.htm.

9.60   This is a particular concern with electrical and electronic goods. In 2000, the European Commission drew attention to the high and increasing cost of waste electrical and electronic equipment.[36] It pointed out that over 90% was landfilled, incinerated or recovered without any pre-treatment, even though it may contain hazardous pollutants. Meanwhile the DTI estimated that, in the UK, households generated 1.1 million tonnes of household electrical and electronic waste in 2007, and this could rise to 1.61 million tonnes in 2017.[37] A proposal which added to this waste would have a negative environmental impact.

9.61   We therefore need to consider carefully whether the existence of the right to reject encourages the disposal of goods which would otherwise be repaired. The issue arises only in relation to high value goods where repair is an economic possibility. In the case of low value items (such as the kettle scenario discussed in the FDS research), repair is not realistic. The choice of remedy is effectively between a refund and a replacement. A replacement which did not meet the consumer's needs would be particularly wasteful. The environmental effect would (if anything) be less if the law were to encourage a refund.

9.62   With regard to high value items, however, it is important not to discourage repairs where they are economically viable. At present, where goods which could be repaired are returned, the retailer may be able to arrange for them to be returned to the manufacturer for remanufacture and subsequent sale. Alternatively, they may be reconditioned by another enterprise or by a not-for-profit organisation.[38]

9.63   Research suggests that the market in remanufactured and reconditioned goods is profitable in the United States, with 73,000 firms operating re-marketing processes, with combined sales of $53 billion a year.[39] The market in the UK is relatively underdeveloped, but has the potential to increase, especially for white goods and electronic products. As the cost of landfill increases, it is expected that the market will develop.[40]

9.64   The market for re-marketed goods, however, becomes more problematic the older the product. Where the consumer has already had considerable use from the product and is returning something which is worn and shabby, the good becomes more difficult to repair and resell. Extending the right to reject may therefore have a negative environmental impact which would need to be considered carefully.

9.65   Finally, we are concerned that extending the right to reject may encourage abuse. Consumers might deliberately break products, or claim that they are faulty, when they were simply unwanted. If such abuse were to occur it would have a negative environmental impact.

---

[36]   See Proposal for a Directive on Waste Electrical and Electronic Equipment, Brussels 13.6.2000, COM (2000) 347 final.

[37]   DTI, WEE Consultation: Final Regulatory Impact Assessment for the WEE Regulations, December 2006.

[38]   DARP (2003) (Devon Appliance Recycling project) Environmental: WEEE Remarket Final Report, 2003, p 95.

[39]   Above, p 93.

[40]   Above, p 93.

Impact on publicly funded advice and assistance

9.66 Our proposals to simplify consumer remedies would have a generally positive impact on advice services. Consumers would feel more confident with the information they had received, and feel less need to talk to an adviser. Consumer advisers could also be trained more easily, and be able to provide shorter, more confident advice.

9.67 In Part 8, we discuss the possibility that notices in shops should say how consumers could obtain further information about their rights. Consumer Direct would appear to be well suited for this task. However, the suggestion has resource implications. It would only be possible if the organisation were provided with sufficient funds to cope with the increased demand on its services. We raise it as an idea, realising that BERR would need to cost the implications of such a proposal before proceeding further.

QUESTIONS

9.68 **We welcome comments and information about the costs and benefits of our proposals.**

9.69 **Do consultees agree that:**

(1) **keeping the current law ("doing nothing") would retain the avoidable administrative burden on retailers and would continue to produce unnecessary disputes?**

(2) **abolishing the right to reject would damage consumer confidence?**

(3) **extending the right to reject would increase costs to business and might lead to increased landfill?**

(4) **the greatest benefits stem from retaining the right to reject but providing appropriate clarification about how it operates?**

PART 10
LIST OF PROVISIONAL PROPOSALS AND QUESTIONS

THE RIGHT TO REJECT IN SALES CONTRACTS

10.1   We provisionally propose that:

   (1)   the right to reject should be retained as a short-term remedy of first instance for consumers. (8.31)

   (2)   the right to reject should not be extended to cover latent defects which appear only after a prolonged period of use. (8.41)

   (3)   the legislation should set out a normal 30-day period during which consumers should exercise their right to reject which would run from the date of purchase, delivery or completion of contract, whichever is later. (8.75)

The normal period of 30 days

10.2   Do consultees agree that 30 days is an appropriate period? We would be interested in receiving arguments for either a shorter or longer period.

10.3   We ask consultees whether it should be open to

   (1)   the retailer to argue for a shorter period where

      (a)   the goods are perishable (that is they are by their nature expected to perish within 30 days)?

      (b)   the consumer should have discovered the fault before carrying out an act inconsistent with returning goods?

   (2)   the consumer to argue for a longer period where

      (a)   it was reasonably foreseeable at the time of sale that a longer period would be needed ("objective circumstances")?

      (b)   the parties agreed to extend the period?

      (c)   the consumer's personal circumstances made it impossible to examine the goods within the 30 day period? If so, should this justify only a short extension, such as an additional 30 days, or a longer extension of six months or more?

      (d)   there were fundamental defects which took time to be discovered?

10.4   Are there are other reasons to justify a shorter or longer period? (8.76 to 8.77)

Other issues

10.5   We provisionally propose that a consumer who exercises a right to reject should be entitled to a reverse burden of proof that the fault was present when the goods were delivered. (8.81)

10.6   We provisionally propose that legal protection for consumers who purchase goods with "minor" defects should not be reduced. (8.91)

THE RIGHT TO REJECT IN OTHER SUPPLY CONTRACTS

10.7   We ask consultees whether the normal 30-day period for rejecting goods should also apply to other contracts for the supply of goods in which property is transferred, or whether the current law should be retained. (8.104)

10.8   We provisionally propose that in hire contracts, the current law should be preserved. When goods develop a fault, the consumer should be entitled to terminate the contract, paying for past hire but not future hire. (8.108)

10.9   We welcome views on the issues raised by hire purchase contracts, and whether they cause any problems in practice. In particular should hire purchase be treated as a supply contract to transfer property in goods, or as analogous to a hire contract? (8.112)

REFORMING THE CONSUMER SALES DIRECTIVE

Clarifying when consumers may proceed to a second tier remedy

The number of repairs

10.10   We provisionally propose that the directive which replaces the CSD should state that after two failed repairs, or one failed replacement, the consumer is entitled to proceed to a second tier remedy. (8.135)

10.11   We provisionally propose that further guidance should be provided stating that the consumer should be entitled to rescind the contract:

(1)   where the product is in daily use, after one failed repair;

(2)   where the product is essential, immediately;

unless the retailer has reduced the inconvenience to the consumer by, for example, offering a temporary replacement. (8.136)

10.12   We welcome views on the form such guidance should take. (8.137)

The process of repairs

10.13   We provisionally propose that there should be best practice guidance on the process of repairing and replacing goods under the CSD (or any replacement to the CSD). (8.141)

10.14   We ask consultees what form that guidance should take. In particular, should it be issued at EU or national level? (8.142)

Dangerous goods and unreasonable behaviour

10.15 We provisionally propose that the CSD should be reformed to allow a consumer to proceed to a second tier remedy when a product has proved to be dangerous or where the retailer has behaved so unreasonably as to undermine trust between the parties. (8.146)

Rescission: the deduction for use

10.16 We ask consultees whether they agree that the "deduction for use" in the event of rescission should be abolished. (8.157)

The six-month reverse burden of proof

10.17 We provisionally propose that the six-month reverse burden of proof should recommence after goods are redelivered following repair or replacement. (8.163)

Time limit for bringing a claim

10.18 We provisionally propose that the time limits for bringing a claim should continue to be those applying to general contractual claims within England, Wales and Scotland. (8.170)

10.19 We welcome views on whether there is a need to prevent consumers from pursuing remedies where faults come to light more than two years after delivery. We welcome views on whether this might cause problems in particular cases. (8.171)

WRONG QUANTITY

10.20 We welcome views on whether there are reasons to retain section 30 of SoGA for consumer sales, or whether cases where the wrong quantity is delivered can be dealt with through the application of general principles. (8.174)

LATE DELIVERY

10.21 We seek consultees' views on whether consumers should be entitled to a full refund whenever the trader fails to meet an agreed delivery date, or whether the current law should be retained. (8.179)

DAMAGES

10.22 We provisionally propose that the right to damages should be retained in UK law. (8.186)

10.23 We seek views on whether the issue of damages should be left to the common law or whether guidance would be helpful on the circumstances in which damages should be payable to consumers. In particular, should damages be available for loss of earnings, distress, disappointment, loss of amenity and inconvenience? If so, for which types of goods, and in which circumstances? (8.187)

INTEGRATION OF CSD REMEDIES WITH THE RIGHT TO REJECT

10.24 We provisionally propose that SoGA and the CSD remedies should be better integrated in a single instrument, by use of the concept of *rejection*. (8.193)

10.25 We provisionally propose that once a consumer has accepted a repair, their right to reject ceases. If the repair fails, the consumer should proceed to a second tier remedy along the lines we have proposed in relation to the reform of the CSD. (8.202)

CONSUMER EDUCATION

10.26 We ask consultees to comment upon how the aim of increasing awareness of consumer legal rights for faulty goods might be achieved. (8.216)

10.27 In particular, should there be a summary of consumer legal rights for faulty goods available at point of sale? If so, which form should it take? (8.217)

10.28 We ask consultees whether they agree that notices displayed in shops should:

(1) use the expression "This does not reduce your legal rights" rather than "This does not affect your statutory rights".

(2) say how a consumer could obtain further information about their legal rights. (8.218)

ASSESSING THE IMPACT OF REFORM

10.29 We welcome comments and information about the costs and benefits of our proposals. (9.68)

10.30 Do consultees agree that:

(1) keeping the current law ("doing nothing") would retain the avoidable administrative burden on retailers and would continue to produce unnecessary disputes?

(2) abolishing the right to reject would damage consumer confidence?

(3) extending the right to reject would increase costs to business and might lead to increased landfill?

(4) the greatest benefits stem from retaining the right to reject but providing appropriate clarification about how it operates? (9.69)

APPENDIX A

QUALITATIVE RESEARCH INTO CONSUMERS' PERCEPTIONS OF CONSUMER REMEDIES FOR FAULTY GOODS

REPORT

PREPARED FOR:

The Law Commission

PREPARED BY:

FDS International Ltd

Hill House

Highgate Hill

London

N19 5NA

Tel: 020 7272 7766

R7451/SG/SL/HG/AR

April 2008

RESEARCH INTO CONSUMERS' PERCEPTIONS
SUMMARY

The Law Commission, and the Scottish Law Commission are undertaking a review of the legal remedies available to customers who have purchased faulty goods.

Qualitative research was carried out to investigate British consumers' perceptions of their legal rights when they buy faulty goods, in particular:-

- whether they are aware of and value the 'right to reject'
- whether they are aware of the time limit of the 'right to reject' and what they feel the time limit should be
- their awareness of the right to replacement/repair
- their reaction to a possible simplification of the law so they would only be entitled to a refund if repair or replacement proved unsatisfactory.

From 18-26 February 2008, eight focus groups and one mini focus group were run with consumers who buy durable goods from shops. Participants ranged in age from 18 upwards and covered social grades A, B, C1, C2 and D (i.e. all but those dependent on state support).

A spread of urban and rural locations in England, Scotland and Wales was used.

Consumers had a partial and flawed understanding of their rights in relation to goods purchased which later proved faulty. Some mistakenly believed they have a good understanding of the law while others admitted ignorance and few participants understood the phrase 'this does not affect your statutory rights'.

The participants aged under 25 in this study appeared likely to underestimate their consumer rights. Older people, often influenced by the policies of their preferred retailers, tended to overestimate their rights. Many older adults, especially, chose to shop where they knew they could return items regardless of faults, and larger chain stores were generally the most accommodating.

Where faults occurred, in most circumstances most consumers would be happy to accept a replacement on the basis they bought the item because they wanted it.

Demanding money back was not widespread although some preferred to receive a credit note and to buy a similar product rather than to receive a like-for-like replacement of an item that had already let them down.

However, while one replacement was generally acceptable, if that replacement also proved faulty people would want and expect to have their money refunded.

Furthermore, while most people would, in the event of a first fault, usually accept replacement or repair instead of a refund, there might be occasions where only a refund would be acceptable. This might apply particularly to an ill-considered purchase of a low value item or to a purchase of a product where the fault gave rise to safety concerns. Therefore, most people would be keen to retain the right to reject, even if some were only vaguely aware of the right and had not recently used it.

People would be sorry to lose the 'right to reject' and feel it is appropriate that it is one of the options available to customers buying faulty goods.

They would be more willing to see the 'right to reject' more tightly defined than to lose it altogether. Currently, virtually no-one is aware customers have a right to refund only a 'reasonable' time after purchase. Some guess around 30 days but others think the 'right to reject' could last a whole year.

While some believe that the period for rejection should be longer for expensive or rarely used items most would be willing to accept a consistent period of around 30 days to reject.

People were generally aware they could ask for a replacement although this would not always be practical if the product was out of stock, especially if the item was bought in a sale.

When problems were found with cars or other high value mechanical or electrical items free repairs were usually seen as the most appropriate solution, but repairs were not wanted nor expected to be offered if a product such as a cheap toaster or kettle proved faulty.

Few were aware that it would be easier to get free repairs or replacement for six months; participants were influenced by manufacturer or retailer warranties, typically expecting these to be offered for twelve months.

And this highlighted how people's expectations of what they will be able to ask for are governed largely by shops' policies rather than by the law. People expect shops to treat them like valued customers and to be very co-operative when they return faulty goods, with shops expected in some cases to be more accommodating than they are legally obliged to be.

There was little awareness of second tier CSD remedies and most found the idea of a partial refund for keeping faulty or damaged goods to be a strange one, although it could be the most mutually beneficial solution if insignificant damage occurred to furniture or electrical items when they were delivered.

If a car developed a recurring fault after several thousand miles some felt the retailer would be justified in making an adjustment for usage, if the customer asked for a refund or replacement. But generally people thought it inappropriate for a retailer to offer less than a 100% refund when a product was returned. It was thought unlikely that reputable retailers would attempt to offer a partial refund for usage, when a customer had been inconvenienced by a faulty product.

Group participants suggested consumer rights, especially changes to them, should be publicised and that key rights and limits to them should be posted in prominent positions in stores.

Yet the impression from these focus groups was that only rarely did lack of understanding of their legal rights really work against these particular consumers. While most were sympathetic to the principle of simplifying the law, confusion surrounding current laws and consumer rights coupled with the policies of retailers to please and appease customers means the current situation can sometimes work to the benefit of consumers.

Stephen Link
Director
April 2008

RESEARCH INTO CONSUMERS' PERCEPTIONS
CONTENTS

INTRODUCTION

The key aims of the Law Commission are:-

- to ensure that the law is as fair, modern, simple and as cost-effective as possible

- to conduct research and consultations in order to make systematic recommendations for consideration by Parliament

- to codify the law, eliminate anomalies, repeal obsolete and unnecessary enactments and reduce the number of separate statutes.

The Law Commission is undertaking a new project, jointly with the Scottish Law Commission, the purpose of which will be to simplify the remedies which are available to customers who have purchased faulty goods. The current law relating to consumer remedies for faulty goods has been criticised for being unnecessarily complex.

The Sale of Goods Act 1979, sets out that goods must:-

- fit the description given

- be of satisfactory quality

- be fit for purpose.

It also requires that faulty goods be returned within a reasonable time frame if the customer is seeking to reject, but the law does not stipulate exactly what 'reasonable' is. For example, what is reasonable in the case of perishable goods could be different for something which is used infrequently.

In 2005, the Chancellor of the Exchequer set up the Davidson Review which concluded that this area of law is overcomplicated because of an unsatisfactory overlap of domestic and EU remedies.

Under the current law, British consumers are able to reject faulty goods and demand a refund in circumstances where, under the EU system, the customer must first seek a repair or replacement.

In November 2007, the Department of Business, Enterprise and Regulatory Reform (DBERR) asked the Law Commission and Scottish Law Commission to undertake a joint project to simplify the law on consumers' remedies for faulty goods.

The argument put forward to support this initiative is that the law relating to consumer remedies for faulty goods is too complex for all parties involved (sales staff, consumers and even consumer advisers) to understand. This can result in customers being dissatisfied, which in turn leads to increased amounts of litigation.

As part of this project, the Law Commission commissioned FDS to undertake qualitative research among consumers to investigate consumers' perceptions of their legal rights when they have bought goods that prove to be faulty.

The key objectives to be met by this study concern consumers' awareness and understanding of this 'right to reject'. In particular, the research was designed to establish:-

- whether UK consumers are actually aware that they may return faulty goods and get their money back – what is known as 'the right to reject'

- whether they are also aware of other rights in connection with faulty goods, such as their right to a replacement or repair

- whether UK consumers use/have ever used the 'right to reject', and what importance they attach to it

- how aware consumers are of a time limit to the 'right to reject', and what they think that limit is/what it should be

- how they would feel if the only circumstances in which they could get their money back would be if either the repair or the replacement was not satisfactory.

This report presents the findings of this qualitative study.

APPROACH

Eight mixed gender focus groups were conducted. The eight groups covered a spread of urban and rural locations with participants of different ages and social grades.

	Location	Social Grade	Age	Date
1	London	C1, C2	25-44	18 February
2	London	A, B, C1	45-74	18 February
3	Carmarthen, Wales	C2, D	25-44	21 February
4	Wimborne, Dorset	A, B, C1	25-44	25 February
5	Newcastle	A, B, C1	18-24	26 February
6	Newcastle	C2, D	45-74	26 February
7	Edinburgh	C1, C2	45-74	26 February
8	Edinburgh	C2, D	25-44	26 February

In addition a mini-group of five A, B and C1 women aged 25-54 was held in north London on 25 February.

Recruitment was undertaken by specialist recruiters from our sister company acefieldwork limited. At the recruitment stage people were excluded if they:-

- or members of their household worked in certain excluded occupations: law, retailing, market research, marketing or journalism
- never bought durable goods or only did through purchasing online
- declare themselves unlikely to ever return items to shops (unless this was due to previous bad experiences of doing so, in which case they would have interesting stories to tell).

In addition, for the eight main focus groups we excluded people who we were concerned might dominate the groups (ie those who had had three or more experiences in the last two years where they found it difficult to get what they wanted when returning faulty items).

We were still interested in the views of such individuals (who appeared to represent well under 10% of all buyers of durable goods and were potentially more extreme in their attitudes and/or behaviour) and recruited five women who had had three or more experiences in the last two years where they found it difficult to get what they wanted when returning faulty items.

During the focus groups participants completed questionnaires regarding what they would do or expect to happen when they encountered problems with durable goods purchased from shops.

Questionnaires used scenarios agreed with the Law Commission which varied slightly from group to group so, for example, those under 25 were given scenarios involving electrical goods rather than household furniture.

In the discussions which preceded and followed the completion of questionnaires moderators explored participants':-

- behaviour and preferences regarding retailers used for durable goods
- experiences of returning faulty goods
- understanding of the law as it stands regarding shoppers' rights in connection with faulty goods
- their views of how the law might be changed and/or simplified
- awareness of and attachment towards the 'right to reject'.

Topic guides were agreed with the Law Commission.

SHOPPERS' EXPERIENCES AND EXPECTATIONS REGARDING FAULTY GOODS

At the start of each focus group we asked participants which stores they preferred when browsing for or buying durable goods such as electrical items, furniture or clothes.

The aim was partly to 'warm up' the group with easy questions each respondent could answer, but also to see to what extent, without any prompting, people mention ease of returning faulty goods as a factor influencing their choice of outlet.

In fact, in every group except the 18-24 year olds, there were several unprompted mentions of ease of returning goods as a factor influencing choice of outlet. This included references to ease of returning faulty goods but for some it was particularly important to be able to take back goods because they had changed their mind. Some clothes retailers did not allow customers to change their mind in this way and hence were avoided by some shoppers.

One particular department store received several mentions in most groups, especially those with older (45+) customers:-

> "Because I'm older and more experienced, I've learned the hard way that [department store name] is the best for big electricals. If there's a problem, [department store name] are the best people to deal with."

A younger female in a Scottish group commented on how the same department store had been very helpful, even giving her a complimentary gift, when she returned a police quad bike which was broken and unusable.

Some shops were considered to be less accommodating and a few customers had found certain specialist electrical retailers to be a little more difficult than other retailers.

Another young Scot observed:-

> "I wouldn't buy from [shop name] again. They were a joke when I took a jacket back. It ripped at the collar. They gave me a replacement and it happened again. I was like sorry I'm not moving until I get my money back. I ended up getting the equivalent of £600 to spend in their shop, that's all they would give me."

In contrast, a shopper at a different high street store recounted returning a leather jacket after years and getting a full refund.

One department store was named by a couple of people to be tough, requiring customers to choose a replacement on the spot if returning faulty goods.

Generally people in the focus groups reported positive experiences of returning faulty goods bought in major chain stores.

The purpose of including these observations is NOT to suggest some major stores are better than others but to highlight that a store's willingness to give refunds or replacements can be one of the factors that determines whether or not someone uses the store.

A helpful policy regarding the return of faulty goods can help a store retain customers and consolidate its own reputation.

Conversely, some are suspicious of and steer clear of small independent outlets partly because they are thought to have or be likely to have less generous policies regarding the return of goods. Some, particularly in Newcastle, were also concerned at the prospect of such stores closing down.

Most group participants had no hesitation in returning faulty goods (and few people dropped out at the recruitment stage on the basis that they were reluctant to take back faulty items).

Across the groups people reported on a wide range of different types of faulty products being returned including:-

- Vehicles
- Computers/printers
- Electrical
- Furniture
- Other household items
- Clothing.

Some recounted experiences of returning products which had never worked while others mentioned products which worked well initially but then broke down – before what they would consider to be the end of a product's life span.

Most people had had some experience of faulty goods. Women appeared a little more likely than men to have taken clothing back and those with the most extensive experience of taking back goods and the most problems doing so were women.

Response to Scenarios – Faulty Kettle

During the course of the focus group people were asked to fill in short questionnaires concerning their understanding of what they are entitled to or what they think should happen when they buy faulty goods.

In each of the groups, some of the participants had experienced a similar circumstance themselves:-

---

SCENARIO
"You buy a kettle at a local shop, but the heating element breaks after one week. The shopkeeper offers a new replacement kettle. Would you accept this? Why?"

The main point of this scenario was to obtain an indication of how many would say they would refuse a replacement (before talking in the group about the right to reject).

In fact around four in five of the people surveyed indicated on their questionnaire that they WOULD accept a replacement kettle. They explained that they would have initially purchased a kettle because they wanted one and assumed the fault was a one-off. In this scenario, people can see the benefit of accepting a replacement – it is easier and more convenient than going to another shop.

However, as well as explaining why they would accept a replacement, all five 'assertive' customers in the mini-group and several others chose to write on their questionnaire that they would want their money back if the fault recurred.

The questionnaires anticipated comments people then made in discussions confirming that if a second fault or a repeat fault occurred people would not want another replacement product but would want their money refunded.

Again, reflecting subsequent discussions, one in five indicated on their questionnaire that even after a single fault they would NOT accept a replacement. Some would be happy with a different product from the same shop but a few would insist on a refund and would then purchase elsewhere.

The minority who would object to receiving the same model of kettle as a replacement expressed a fear that the product had a fault that would recur in other kettles:-

"I'd have lost trust in the kettle."

"If the first one broke there's every chance the second will do the same."

"I would be entitled to my money back."

Subsequent discussions revealed that people would be more likely to accept a replacement kettle (rather than a refund) if they had made a very considered decision to buy that particular model in the first place. If it was a well known brand, a distinctive model or a highly priced product they would be more likely to want a replacement, believing the fault to be a one-off and being keen to have the product they had carefully selected:-

"I'd say 'yes' if I really, really wanted that particular model."

"I was hoping that they would replace it. I was quite happy for a replacement because I chose that model."

"I said that if it were a brand that I knew and trusted then I'd accept that the original one had a fault. However, I would specify that if it were to happen again, I would demand a refund."

Where people had made a less considered decision as to which model to buy, especially where they had purchased a less-well known or cheaper make, they would be more likely to expect faults to recur in any replacement they were given and hence to want their money back or to receive a credit note rather than to have a replacement kettle:-

"No, not the same brand. Not the same one. I bought a kettle at [shop name] just before Christmas and the thing was leaking all over the place. It was one of their own and I took it back. They offered me a replacement of the same one and I said 'no'."

And many were aware that they could demand a refund when goods proved faulty:-

"If it's faulty, I think you'd be entitled to a refund but I think if you didn't like it then I understand like a credit note or something but if the item is faulty or broke or whatever I believe regardless of what it is you are entitled to a full refund."

Some were doubtful as to whether they would still be entitled to a refund if the shop had a notice at the till saying "no refund". People thought that would only apply to customers who changed their minds but some were not sure on this point.

Response to Scenarios – Faulty Car

The third scenario that people answered was similar to the kettle problem but:-

- involved a much more expensive purchase
- the item itself was still useable though not functioning properly
- questions related to what people thought they were entitled to rather than what they would be willing to accept.

SCENARIO

"You buy a new car and a week later, the power steering pump stops working so you take the car back to the garage. Are you entitled to a full refund of the car, a new car of the same model or to require the retailer to repair the fault."

Only 34% of those completing questionnaires thought they were entitled to receive a full refund. Almost half (46%) thought they could insist on returning the car and receiving a new car of the same model.

Most (71%) wrote that they could require the retailer to repair the fault though interestingly, significant numbers did not think this was the case.

In discussions people tended to agree that the value of the item purchased should not dictate what customers were entitled to when there were problems with the product.

When they tried to consider the subject logically they thought that if one would be entitled to a refund if a cheap kettle proved faulty, the same would be true if an expensive car proved faulty.

However, the much higher cost of a new car led many to expect different solutions from those available to the kettle purchaser.

For example, a young man in the London group argued that when you spend tens of thousands on a new car *"you're buying into a contract and that's where I don't think refunds apply for things like cars"*.

Whereas repairs were thought to be often impractical and not worth the effort on low value items, realistically, in the scenarios described, or when other problems occurred with cars, most would expect the car to be repaired.

In the scenario of a power steering pump not working or a similar repairable fault most would not expect to be offered a refund and did not think they could demand one.

They also felt the garage would probably not offer a replacement, at least not initially.

If a fault was continuous or kept recurring the situation might change and the customer would be more likely to be offered a replacement but this is not something people would generally initially expect – although almost half thought they would be entitled to receive a new car of the same model in the event of the power steering failure.

In discussions relating to this scenario it was clear people were influenced by manufacturers' warranties and guarantees rather than their understanding of the law.

Some who thought they would be entitled to ask for a new car would nevertheless expect to accommodate the retailer to some extent in giving them a chance to put right a fault.

However, a serious fault, especially one that was potentially dangerous for the driver and their passengers could destroy confidence in a make and model so in these instances, some customers felt they should be entitled to a refund rather than replacement or repair.

In the case of replacement or refund some acknowledged that the situation might be complicated by the fact that once the car has been driven it would have depreciated in value and this might affect the size of the refund. However, people questioned how you could quantify an appropriate reduction especially as drivers differed greatly in how they drove and looked after their cars. Furthermore as the customer would have been inconvenienced by series of problems with their car it would be fairer to give them a new replacement or a full refund.

Two participants had interesting and somewhat worrying experiences regarding faulty new cars:

A London woman had a problem with the brakes on her three-month old car which continued for a further six months. Eventually, after a series of unsuccessful or only partially successful repairs, the vehicle breakdown recovery company, (who had been called out fourteen times), sent an engineer's report to the manufacturer and the car was replaced with a brand new one.

Most worryingly the vehicle breakdown recovery company told her that the problem with the brakes that she had experienced while driving on the motorway, was common for that model.

The woman asked for her money back (although the fault did not occur until she had had the car for three months). She ended up swapping her brand new replacement car for a new car from a different manufacturer as she had lost all confidence in that make of car.

Two months after purchase an older man in Newcastle had a problem with his car's electric windows going down of their own accord, resulting in its interior getting wet.

After this problem occurred a fourth time the exasperated driver:-

> *"Phoned up the consumer advice people and they said as this was the fourth time they should give them four or five chances to fix it. They said write a registered letter saying you are not happy, you will take the car somewhere else, get it fixed, pay for it, and claim the price off them.*

> *They said I could demand a car of the same value but as it had done 7,000 miles take that off a replacement car."*

Response to Scenarios – retailer's 30 day money back guarantee

In six of the main groups participants were faced with a scenario featuring a washing machine which crucially made reference to the shop's own guarantee.

"You buy a washing machine in a local shop. The shop has a '30 day no quibble money back guarantee'. After you use the washing machine, the drum breaks, under current laws are you eligible for:-

A)   **a full refund**
B)   **a replacement washing machine**
C)   **free repair of the washing machine**

and if so, for how long after purchase would that right last for?"

Under current law, ignoring retailers' or manufacturers' guarantees, the customer is entitled to replacement or free repairs for six months.

The retailer's statement means the customer is entitled to a refund for 30 days but it could be argued that in the case of a washing machine with numerous washing cycles the 'reasonable' period in which a customer can expect a legal right to a refund should be longer, perhaps six weeks.

Not surprisingly, almost all of the 46 participants thought they were entitled to all three remedies if it broke down within 30 days:-

- full refund (96% of those answering)

- replacement washing machine (92%)

- free repair of washing machine (95%).

Most were very familiar with the concept of a 30 day no quibble money back guarantee.

This was seen as particularly beneficial if they were buying an item they were unsure about.

They understood that a no quibble money back guarantee would enable them to return articles for any reason, and without giving a reason within the specified period. After 31 days it would be more difficult, and perhaps not possible to return something simply on the basis they did not like it or had changed their mind.

Older respondents, especially, were influenced by their expectation that white goods, indeed almost all electrical goods, would have manufacturers' guarantees of at least 12 months so some thought the retailer's guarantee was somewhat redundant where faults were concerned.

However, some respondents, especially those in Scotland and Wales, appeared to have been influenced by the shop's own 30 day guarantee when asked for how long they would have the right to demand a refund or replacement for a faulty washing machine. We are NOT suggesting that Scottish/Welsh people in general are more likely than English people to be influenced in this way, simply reporting differences found in the groups we conducted.)

While some correctly identified that a right to a full refund did not last as long as the right to replacement, others underestimated the length of the right to replacement believing it to be only 30 days.

The effect of a retailer's own guarantee may, therefore, encourage people to underestimate their rights especially because, as we shall see later, people do not understand the meaning of phrases such as "This does not affect your statutory rights".

When asked how long they thought their right to a full refund would last, almost all the participants in the Welsh group and the two Scottish groups thought it would only last 30 days. In the three English groups people were more evenly divided between those who thought it would last twelve months and those who thought it would last 30 days. A few felt unable to answer and one suggested 90 days.

The pattern was slightly different when those who thought they were entitled to a replacement considered how long that right would last for.

About a third suggested thirty days (including two individuals who wrote "28 days").

Some suggested answers of more than one month but less than one year, such as 90 days or three months or "a few months". Three Londoners correctly wrote six months. One suggested "a reasonable period" or that it depends on the retailer, whilst a couple suggested that it would depend on the guarantee/warranty. The most common answer suggested by around a half of those answering was 12 months.

Similarly about half those who thought they were entitled to free repairs suggested this right would last for twelve months.

A few Welsh and Scottish participants suggested this right would last only thirty days whilst one Londoner suggested "a short while after buying" and another, six months.

Almost a third of participants wrote in that it would depend on the guarantee/warranty for how long one would be entitled to free repair.

Answers are summarised in the table below:-

Table 3.1: Perceptions of how long rights last			
	Full refund	Replacement	Free repair
30 days	Two thirds	One third	Very few
One year	One third	One half	One half
Depends on guarantee	Very few	Few	One third
Other answers			Very few

The key messages are:-

- (possibly influenced by guarantees and expectations that washing machines would last several years) some expected a full refund for at least twelve months

- several individuals DID give different answers for refund v replacement or repair suggesting the right to refund was for a shorter period

- sizeable numbers underestimated the length of period of which they are entitled to replacement

- very few thought that the period for replacement or repair is six months. People were clearly influenced by 12 month guarantees – they expected to be covered for labour for a minimum of a year.

Given the price of washing machines and the potential hassle involved in getting a replacement, people tended to expect the retailer to arrange repairs when possible. As a Welsh woman suggested:-

> *"I think most of the time if things are like under £100 they tend to just take it back and give you a new one. Like a washing machine you are talking £200 odd. So they're going to think, ah, that's a bit expensive like, so we'll try and fix that one first."*

People would want repairs carried out quickly, especially to an important product like a washing machine, that some families might use (almost) every day.

Some initially felt it was unreasonable to wait more than a day for repairs but might be prepared to accept three days especially if any expenditure in a launderette was met while their washing machine was out of action. When talking about a reasonable length of time for repairs, one consumer said:

> *"'Reasonable' should be based on the number of uses rather than reasonable length of time – you could be using it every day."*

Some would be happy to wait three days while some might accept seven or even ten days for their washing machine to be repaired. Having a convenient and fixed appointment time was important for some.

In the two Newcastle groups and the London mini-group with frequent returners a similar scenario was presented, but this time involving a digital camera rather than a washing machine.

> **"You buy a digital camera in a local shop. The shop has a '30 day no quibble money back guarantee'. After you use the camera, the screen on the back breaks. Under current law are you entitled to:-**
>
> **a) a full refund**
> **b) a replacement**
> **c) free repair**
> **and if so, for how long after purchase would that right last for?"**

Interestingly, in an earlier London group, a man had a problem with a digital camera but when he took it back, the shopkeeper said he must have dropped it:-

> *"This was a shop in Tottenham Court Road which I don't use any more for that reason. I stuck to my guns and eventually they grudgingly gave me another one."*

This scenario proved less clear cut than the washing machine scenario because some participants thought such a fault would have been visible at the time of purchase or if it was not, thought they might have caused the screen on the back to break, or have difficulty convincing the retailer that they had not caused the problem:-

> *"I wouldn't take it back because I would think they'd think it is me – that I'd dropped it."* (18-24)

> *"I was out on a night out and it got whacked and I woke up in the morning and it had a big crack so I thought there's no way they'll take that back. So I went and bought another one."* (18-24 describing an actual experience)

> *"I'd say yes (a full refund) – but then it depends how it breaks."*
> (frequent returner)

The result was that several of the 23 participants did not think they were entitled to a full refund or repairs.

Of the 17 (74%) who did, the under 25s tended to think the period would last for 30 days while older adults usually suggested 12 months, although some proposed 30 days.

In the under 25s group only five of the nine participants thought the customer would be entitled to a refund (including two who thought the customer would be entitled to a refund but NOT a replacement).

They may have been influenced by a feeling that if something had broken their actions would have caused it.

But in suggesting their rights only last 30 days they again underestimated their rights (this time influenced by the retailer's money back guarantee).

Twenty-one out of 23 thought they were entitled to a replacement with under 25s again tending to favour 30 days while older respondents usually answered 12 months.

Eighteen out of 21 who answered thought they were entitled to a repair, and almost all the over 25s thought this would be for one year, although the under 25s still tended to answer "30 days" or "depends on the guarantee".

Response to Scenarios – Gift not opened until two months after purchase

The fourth scenario asked people to consider what the law SHOULD be rather than what it actually says:-

> **"In October you buy a teddy bear as a present for your niece. When she opens her present on Christmas Day morning and hugs the teddy the seams rip open and the stuffing comes out."**

Regardless of what the law actually is, almost everyone (54 out of 63) believed one should be entitled to a refund or a replacement.

One of the few to say "no" explained that she thought the product should be taken off the market if more than one customer had this experience.

It was clear from comments made in groups, especially by women aged 40 or above, that some retailers were already making allowances for this kind of eventuality and some "shopping savvy" participants always asked the retailer for a gift receipt to cover them:-

> *"Presuming it was for Christmas, you'd ask the girl behind the till to say it was for Christmas."*

> *"Most places ask you. I found this year – lots of people asked is this for Christmas – so do you want a receipt for Christmas. And then they write on it – we've got until 23 January or something like that."*

Other people gave other examples of delays between purchasing and giving a gift or delays between purchasing and using an item.

For example, some said one could get bargains on seasonal wear out of season or at the end of a season, so one might buy ski wear at lower prices in the summer. This was seen as potentially more complicated than purchasing a Christmas present a few months early.

While people felt a refund should still be offered if an item proved not fit for purpose it was thought that it might be more difficult, although others pointed out that it would be obvious to the retailer when you bought it that you were not likely to use it for months.

Sometimes people buy items they don't immediately need but take advantage of a special offer or buy several products in one trip to save going back to a particular store.

So a Newcastle man who bought an electric saw he did not then use for six weeks insisted (and eventually obtained) a refund when it proved faulty.

WHAT CONSUMERS WANT

Before informing people what their rights were, we explored more fully what they actually wanted.

As was apparent from the kettle scenario, replacement is often the preferred option.

In most circumstances, most customers would accept a replacement or repair rather than insisting on a refund. They did, after all, buy a product because they needed one. So if a toaster or kettle breaks they will need another one.

A refund may involve more hassle than a replacement as the customer then has to go to another shop to find a product.

People are especially likely to want and/or to accept a replacement where the item:-

- was chosen after much thought
- was a well known and/or expensive brand.

So, for example, a young London man described how he was willing to undergo a degree of inconvenience to replace a pair of shoes he really liked:-

> *"They had to order in a new pair. I think it was the one in Oxford Street and they were the only ones that actually stocked them. So they had to order a pair and it took about five days. I liked the fit and everything else so I just thought rather than buying another pair and not liking them as much as these ones, I thought why not try it. If they didn't have the same ones then I would probably have got a refund."* (Although he had had the shoes over a month so might have been unsuccessful in asking for a refund).

However, as we found in the kettle scenario, a significant minority of customers would be unhappy to be offered a replacement of the same model. Their confidence in the product would have been damaged, and they would fear that the replacement would develop a similar problem, requiring them to face the inconvenience of taking that back too.

Some faults, such as stitching coming away in clothes, incline the purchaser to think the same problem will occur with replacements so there may be some purchases where many or even most customers would prefer a refund to replacement. Faults that are potentially dangerous or hazardous are likely to fall into this category.

And some respondents gave the impression they would lose interest or enjoyment in a product that had actually failed them once.

One young London woman who often regretted purchases she had made on a whim admitted taking advantage of faults to get her money back on things she had not been keen to keep anyway. She was keen to have a right to reject.

However, in most circumstances the majority would be happy to accept a replacement but if that replacement proved unsatisfactory a refund would be asked for and expected. People would not expect to be required to test a third product nor happy to do so.

Repairs were seen to be much more relevant for high value than low value items. Repairs were thought to be unlikely to be even offered in the case of low value goods where the labour costs involved might exceed the price of the product.

Expectations regarding high value items were different and this was highlighted when people talked about cars, washing machines or other white goods.

Where a fault with a car is essentially cosmetic, or does not affect its safety people are happy to give the car retailer the opportunity to put it right:-

> *"I think with a car – obviously it takes so much longer to build – there's so much more stuff that goes into it and it's just one element of this massive manufactured thing which costs a lot of money – then they're likely to offer to repair the one little bit."*

If a fault meant driving the car was potentially dangerous some participants would be unhappy with a repair, preferring to receive a replacement car, or even, if their confidence had been rocked to that extent, a refund.

This study is qualitative in nature and caution should be exercised in assuming that differences found between different demographics in our focus groups will be replicated on a wider scale.

Nevertheless, there was evidence from these groups that men are more likely to be willing to accept replacements/repairs than women. It also appeared that the most "assertive" customers tended to be women and this seemed to be only partly due to them buying more different items than men and hence having more experience of taking items back.

We also found our group of under 25s in Newcastle were a little more willing to see issues from the retailer's viewpoint and less confident of their rights than the over 25s especially those over 45. Again as a generalisation we found those most likely to overstate their rights were over 45s, especially women.

They were more inclined to effectively ignore their legal rights and to base their expectations of what they were entitled to and what they would receive on the precedent set by large retailers when they or people they knew had taken goods back in the past.

While not actually using the phrase "the customer is always right" some respondents, especially some of the middle-aged or older women appeared to think or act in this way or expect department store staff to take this view.

ROLE OF LAW

It was apparent from the questionnaires and the discussion that very few people have a clear idea of what the law states. One of those with a reasonable understanding was a young man in Newcastle who had briefly studied law but he was in a small minority.

He remembered that consumer rights all begin with the letter "R" but could not remember what each one was, although he did get the answers to most scenarios right.

Another participant, a woman who frequently returned goods, mentioned specifically the term 'right to reject':-

> *"That says – I bought these goods, they don't do what they're supposed to do, I'd like my money please."*

Sometimes people's understanding of the law appeared to be influenced by the policies of the retailers or manufacturers they favoured, and by what retailers told them:-

> *"You wouldn't need to think about your legal rights if they're telling you."*

> *"Nobody in the room kens their legal rights so you're led by the shop."*

The law was less important in determining what would happen when they returned faulty goods than the retailer's wish to:-

- retain the goodwill of the customer in question and give them confidence when making future purchases

- avoid arguments with customers in the shops

- avoid adverse publicity or word of mouth, and perhaps to benefit from favourable word of mouth.

Some participants believe that operating in competitive markets where shoppers are able to choose where to shop and which brands to buy compels retailers to adopt customer-friendly policies regarding the return of goods.

Customers may benefit from retailers' eagerness to retain their goodwill, but they may also accept what a retailer tells them their policy is, even if this is less generous to the customer than the law.

For example, many believe that without a receipt they have little chance of a refund even if they return a product in its original packaging.

A few had talked of reporting poor practices to Trading Standards but they felt that the law would only become involved if they had to have recourse to the Small Claims Court to obtain what they thought they were entitled to from a recalcitrant retailer.

One of the most striking findings is that people had heard of but did not understand the phrase "this does not affect your statutory rights".

Few participants were even willing to volunteer suggestions as to what it meant and sometimes those who did were widely inaccurate. A Londoner thought it was to do with a person's credit rating.

These responses from 25-44 year old Scots were typical:-

> *"Haven't got a clue."*
> *"I don't know what they are."*
> *"I just kind of always ignore that bit."*
> *"What does it mean? Small Claims Court?"*
> *"It means your rights as a consumer but you don't know what they are."*

Some decided the term related to your right to receiving money back if something is not fit for purpose "no matter what's written on the wall of the store".

The full focus group with the highest proportion knowing or guessing correctly what the term meant was 18-24 year olds in Newcastle, three out of nine of them giving reasonable explanations. Thus in all the demographic groups covered, most are unaware of what the phrase means.

In several groups, people suggested consumer rights and limitations on these should be publicised, but some admitted that they would never study notices in shops even if prominently displayed, partly because they did not want to have negative thoughts when making a purchase.

SECOND TIER CSD REMEDIES – PARTIAL REFUND

The final scenario was introduced after people had been told that they would normally be entitled to:-

- a refund if the faulty item was returned to the shop within 'a reasonable time'

- a replacement or free repair if the product was brought back within six months (or longer if the customer could prove the product was faulty when purchased).

The two Newcastle groups answered questions about a TV that was still usable but was not working as it should.

> **"You buy a TV. After 7 weeks the on/off button on the TV stops working so you can only turn it off at the socket. You can still put it on standby from the remote control."**

The first half of this scenario asked people what they thought they were entitled to and introduced the idea of people receiving a reduction in price if they kept the TV despite the fact it was not functioning as it should.

Only one individual out of 18 thought they were entitled to a reduction in the price if they kept the TV.

Eight out of 18 believed they were entitled to a full refund if they returned the TV (though this would probably only be true if they had a guarantee to this effect) while almost all (16 out of 18) stated correctly they would be able to demand a new replacement TV.

It was interesting to see how answers changed when people were asked to assume that the replacement they accepted also proved faulty.

In these circumstances all eighteen thought they would be entitled to a full refund if they returned the TV. Echoing earlier comments, they thought it would be unfair not to give this option to a customer who had already been inconvenienced.

Interestingly, only half thought the customer would be entitled to another (ie a second) replacement TV, fewer than thought they could insist on a replacement after the first problem.

Given the fact the original TV had only been used for seven weeks and the second an unspecified length of time it is perhaps unsurprising that all thought a full refund was due and nobody thought the customer was only entitled to a partial refund, making allowance for the use they had had.

One person thought they would be entitled to a reduction in price if they kept the TV. In the discussion which followed it became clear this was not an attractive option as people wanted a fully functioning TV.

Some of the other groups were given a similar scenario this time concerning a discoloured table.

> **"You buy a dining table from a furniture shop. After 8 weeks the varnish is beginning to change colour and the table looks ugly. You have done nothing unusual with the table."**

The pattern of responses was generally similar to the TV example.

The numbers believing one would be entitled to a full refund were half (18 out of 36) on the first occasion there was a problem, rising to 26 out of 36 (72%) in the event that they were given a replacement which also proved faulty.

Most (30 out of 36) believed they would be entitled to a new replacement table, but numbers dropped to just 20 out of 36 in the event of a problem with the replacement.

Initially six people thought they might be entitled to a reduction in price if they were to keep the table, dropping to three out of thirty six (8%) in the event of a recurrence of the problem.

Only one person thought they were entitled to a partial refund only, reflecting the use they had, if they chose to take product back. The idea of a partial refund was a strange concept to most participants.

The main relevant experience some people have is buying something damaged at a reduced price but in this instance people would be aware of the problem at the time of purchase.

A close parallel would be people having white goods or furniture damaged on delivery and accepting some money off.

If the damaged area was not normally visible this solution could be attractive to the customer who has their product at a reduced price, and this option is far less unattractive to the retailer than options requiring the item to be taken away again.

A woman in the older Newcastle group was very pleased to accept £50 off a bed when one of the drawers, which would not normally be visible, was slightly damaged when it arrived.

However, most participants would be very reluctant to keep an item like a dining table which did not look good, although some might be willing to keep it covered by a tablecloth.

Similarly, if they had bought an electrical item, most would be keen that it was fully functional and would not be interested in a refund to compensate them for it not working fully.

In the case of a damaged table or a less than fully functional electrical item a partial refund was seen by most as unsatisfactory – it simply was not what they wanted.

While the idea of keeping the product but receiving some money off was not popular, people could easily see the logic behind it, and could conceive circumstances where this would satisfy retailer and customer.

A more alien concept related to returning goods and receiving a refund less a certain percentage to allow for use made of the product.

Participants struggled to see how it would work, and were highly dubious of how such a concept could be framed in law, rather than something agreed between consumer and retailer.

> *"I don't know anyone that's done it because you've got to be able to negotiate haven't you – and there can't be a law to say how much. It really is discretional."*

Some people objected to this idea on principle or on grounds of fairness, arguing that if through no fault of the customer, a product proves to be faulty, that customer should not lose part of their refund.

Taking products back to shops and being without them while they are repaired or replaced can be a hassle and inconvenient to customers.

Some think there is a stronger case for compensating the customer for their inconvenience than reducing the money they are refunded on the basis that they obtained some use from the product.

This idea seemed to be weighted heavily in the retailer's favour at the expense of the consumer and of the spirit of fair play.

However, where the value of a product had gone down as a result of being used (as in the case of a car depreciating in value) some could see a partial refund being appropriate. The value of that refund would be calculated more fairly on the basis of the car having driven x of its expected y total mileage which might then represent a reduction of 5% or less.

Where the consumer was blameless and there was a fault with the car it would seem unfair to penalise the customer by the amount the car had depreciated since leaving the showroom.

In the younger Newcastle group some were aware of friends or other young people who returned products frivolously, for example, after wearing clothes a few times. By constantly asking for replacements on tenuous grounds some shoppers were able to effectively have a series of new items of clothing for the price of a single item.

But one of the strongest arguments against this idea was that large customer-friendly retailers with reputations to maintain would not want to give anything less than a full refund to a customer who had twice had problems with items purchased.

Participants did not think retailers would want to haggle or give less than a full refund where customers encountered problems.

Giving a partial refund was thought to be potentially damaging to a retailer's reputation and inconsistent with their desire to please customers and compete effectively with like-minded outlets.

REFORMING THE RIGHT TO REJECT

While unlikely to use the phrase 'right to reject' many were aware that in certain situations they could demand to have their money back. However, for some, the fact that they were able to do this was tied in with guarantees or retailers' policies rather than their legal rights, so if retailer policies were guaranteed to remain unaltered participants might not be too concerned at a change in their legal rights.

A minority of participants were unaware of or had never exercised the 'right to reject' and hence were unconcerned at the prospect of losing it:-

> *"I've never been in that situation. I've never asked for my money back. They've always said do you want a replacement?"* (Newcastle, older female).

A male in this group had very rarely encountered problems and the group started to agree that they would not really mind if the 'right to reject' was lost, but examples were thrown in of when it might be needed, and gradually the group reverted to opposing the potential loss of the 'right to reject'.

Other groups did not even get close to accepting the loss of the 'right to reject'. Most participants were reluctant to lose the 'right to reject'. There are situations where a refund is the only acceptable option – and this may be after 4-6 weeks. In the kettle scenario, we saw a significant minority of one in five reject the notions of replacement or repair.

People thought the likelihood of problems being found with a product were greater where that same model had already developed a fault. Some did not want to risk having to face the hassle of taking back products for the second time:-

> *"The goods are broken. I lead a busy, busy life. I don't want to have to keep going backwards and forwards, and then after the second time, you're very generously saying 'have your money back' I don't want to be doing all that. I might want the money back straightforward because the fault is not mine."* (London, older female).

People were in almost universal agreement that in most circumstances, if a customer was unhappy with their replacement or repair then they must be able to have a refund, and people saw a full refund as fairer and more appropriate than a partial refund:-

> *"Fine-but if it happens again, then you are entitled to a full refund."*

> *"A replacement is fine and a repair is fine, then you get to the point where you think-no, this is just not on."*

It was clear from the discussions that few people had a clear idea of the time during which goods could be returned – and the clear views of some individuals differed from the views of others.

Some participants assumed the time during which goods could be returned equated to the minimum life span of the products so this might be:-

- 3 years for large white goods, such as washing machines

- 12 months for small electrical goods, such as kettles or toasters

- but generally a shorter time for clothing, especially if cheap.

But others took a different view and thought that to obtain a refund, 28-30 days was the usual period and this message was often on the reverse of a receipt.

Opinions differed regarding what the law currently was.

When it was explained that people can obtain a refund when goods are returned within a 'reasonable time', which was often four weeks for simple products, opinions varied as to whether this was reasonable.

Some felt 30 days was almost always adequate – particularly when they had been told that the customer would still be entitled to free repairs or replacement if the item is taken back within six months. Others, influenced by the expected life span of products and typical warranty periods argued for a longer period.

Some could see benefits in having a standard period during which items could be returned regardless of type of product or level of usage. Others argued that the time period should vary by:-

- type of product (with the period generally longer for more valuable and less frequently used products)

- how long the product is expected to last, so an item expected to last several years could legitimately have a longer period in which it could be returned than one expected to last several months

- how much the product had been used (so a kettle used constantly in a workplace could not be expected to last as long in calendar terms as one used a few times a day at home)

- and indeed this also tied in with the issue of products purchased but not used, and not expected to be used for several months

- the cost of the product, so refunds would be expected over a longer period for high value than low value items.

"You don't expect a refund after a time unless it's really expensive."

Nevertheless, people would be much happier with a standardised period of say, 30 days, where they had the right to reject, than the possibility of losing this right altogether.

ANNEX 1: PRE-DISCUSSION QUESTIONNAIRE

Q1.   You buy a kettle at a local shop, but the heating element breaks after one week. You take it back and the shopkeeper offers you a new replacement kettle.

Would you accept a replacement kettle? (PLEASE TICK YOUR ANSWER)

Yes
No

PLEASE EXPLAIN YOUR ANSWER

Q2.   You buy a washing machine in a local shop. The shop has a "30 day no quibble money back guarantee". After you use the washing machine, the drum breaks. Under current law:

a)   Are you entitled to a full refund for the washing machine?
YES/NO (TICK ONE)
If yes, how long after purchase would that right last for?

b)   Are you entitled to a replacement washing machine? YES/NO
If yes, how long after purchase would that right last for?

c)   Are you entitled to a repair of the washing machine free of charge? YES/NO
If yes, how long after purchase would that right last for?

Q3.   You buy a new car and a week later, the power steering pump stops working so you take the car back to the garage.

Are you entitled to... TICK ANY THAT APPLY

a)   Return the car and receive a full refund for the car?

b)   Return the car and receive a new one of the same model?

c)   Require the retailer to repair the fault?

Q4. In October you buy a teddy bear as a present for your niece. When she opens her present on Christmas Day morning and hugs the teddy the seams rip open and the stuffing comes out.

   a) Regardless of what the law actually is...SHOULD the law entitle you to a full refund? YES/NO (TICK ONE)

   b) SHOULD the law entitle you to a new teddy bear? YES/NO

Q5. You buy a dining table from a furniture shop. After 8 weeks the varnish is beginning to change colour, and the tabletop looks ugly. You have done nothing unusual with the table. Which of the following do you think you are entitled to? Tick those that apply.

   a) A full refund if you return the table.

   b) A new replacement table.

   c) A reduction in the price if you keep the table.

   If you accept a replacement and that also proves to be faulty, which of the following do you think you are entitled to? Tick any that apply.

   a) A full refund if you return the table.

   b) A partial refund if you return the table, to allow for the use you have had of the table.

   c) Another new replacement table

   d) A reduction in price if you keep the table.

ANNEX 2: PRE-DISCUSSION QUESTIONNAIRE (FOR THE YOUNGER GROUP)

Q1.   You buy a kettle at a local shop, but the heating element breaks after one week. You take it back and the shopkeeper offers you a new replacement kettle.

Would you accept a replacement kettle? (PLEASE TICK YOUR ANSWER)

Yes
No

PLEASE EXPLAIN YOUR ANSWER

Q2.   You buy a digital camera in a local shop. The shop has a "30 day no quibble money back guarantee". After you use the camera, the screen on the back breaks. Under current law:

a)   Are you entitled to a full refund for the camera? YES/NO (TICK ONE)
If yes, how long after purchase would that right last for?

b)   Are you entitled to a replacement camera? YES/NO
If yes, how long after purchase would that right last for?

c)   Are you entitled to a repair of the camera free of charge? YES/NO
If yes, how long after purchase would that right last for?

Q3.   In October you buy a teddy bear as a present for your niece. When she opens her present on Christmas Day morning and hugs the teddy the seams rip open and the stuffing comes out.

a)   Regardless of what the law actually is...SHOULD the law entitle you to a full refund? YES/NO (TICK ONE)

b)   SHOULD the law entitle you to a new teddy bear? YES/NO

Q4.   You buy a TV. After 7 weeks the on/off button on the TV stops working, so you can only turn it off at the socket. You can still put it on standby from the remote control. You have done nothing unusual with the TV in those 7 weeks. Which of the following do you think you are entitled to? Tick those that apply.

a)   A full refund if you return the TV.

b)   A new replacement TV.

c)   A reduction in the price if you keep the TV.

If you accept a replacement and that also proves to be faulty, which of the following do you think you are entitled to? Tick any that apply.

a)   A full refund if you return the TV.

b)   A partial refund if you return the TV, to allow for the use you have had of the table.

c)   Another new replacement TV

d)   A reduction in price if you keep the TV.

ANNEX 3: RESEARCH INTO SHOPPERS' PERCEPTIONS TOPIC GUIDE

Introduction

- Welcome
- Briefly explain purpose of research and housekeeping
- Individuals introduce themselves
  - brief personal details plus which shop they are most likely to buy from
  - does ability to take goods back influence their choice of shop or are all stores pretty much the same

Complete Questionnaire (Qs1-4)

- Has anyone had a problem like these in recent months
- If so, what did they WANT to happen when they went back to shop
  - and what ACTUALLY happened
  - (if different) were they happy with this? Why?

- Generally was the questionnaire easy or difficult to fill in? If difficult is this because the law is complicated or because they are simply not aware of the law. Is it more important that the law is simple and clear or that consumers rights are given the maximum possible protection

TURN TO QUESTIONNAIRE – Q1

- Would anyone NOT accept a replacement kettle? Why not? What would they want instead? Would they be entitled to refuse a replacement kettle? So when are people entitled to ask for their money back?

TURN TO Q3

- A car is a much more expensive item. So do the same laws apply to a car as to a lower value item? Would they prefer refund, replacement or repairs? Why? How many think they are ENTITLED to
  - full refund
  - replacement
  - free repairs
  On what do they base this view?

What if they were only entitled to replacement or repairs? Would this be fair/reasonable?

TURN TO Q2

- What do they understand by the term "*30 day no quibble money back guarantee*"? In general would they rely on retailers' return policies or their legal rights?
- What do they understand by the phrase "*this does not affect your statutory rights*"
- So for how long after purchase would they be entitled to a full refund? On what is their view based? What would be fair for the customer? And for the retailer? Would six weeks be reasonable? What about six months?

- Are they entitled to a replacement/free repair? For how long ARE they entitled to replacement? What is fair? Would six weeks be reasonable? What about six months? What about a year?

TURN TO Q4

- What if a product is not used until some time after it is brought (eg Ski equipment bought in the Summer)? Should it make a difference whether or not the customer tells the retailer the item will not be used for months after purchase?

- Should the length of time people are allowed to reject an item and ask for a refund be fixed

    - should it be the same for all products?

    - how should the length of time be determined?

    - should it be based on the customer having a reasonable opportunity to identify a problem?

- EXPLAIN English/Scottish Law currently entitles to refund, replacement or repair - and that they have the right to reject a faulty product.

- Anyone surprised at this?

- Is this fair?

- Is giving customers three options too complicated or simply being fair to them?

- The time period for rejection is based on a reasonable time e.g. how long it would take to road test the goods. This is different from the 6 months for repairs/replacement. Is this fair/reasonable/understandable? What would be reasonable?

- Do they think retailers attempt to claim back money lost through refunds by raising prices? Or does this make no difference?

- How important is the right to reject? How often would people expect to use this rather than accept repair/replacement?

- What if the only option available were replacement or repair and that the right to reject be removed

    - but with the option to reject if replacement also prove faulty?

Would this be fair? In what circumstances would it be unacceptable? Should the same rules apply to all types of product and all types of fault?

Complete Q5 of Questionnaire.

Did anyone think they were entitled to a price reduction for keeping the table? How attractive would this option be? Why? What sort of reduction might they expect? Have they ever been offered or asked for this option? Did they agree a reduction? How satisfactory was this option?

- What about the idea of a partial refund if they return the table? What sort of refund would they expect (eg 80%/90% of sale price) Have they ever been offered or asked about this option? What do people feel about the principle of a partial refund taking into account usage?

- Should the refund be linked to expected life of product? Is this a practical option? Would they expect to have to negotiate with a retailer or could clear guidelines be established?
- Does the idea of partial refunds give a better balance between consumers and retailer rights than a simple right to reject?
- What do they think is the fairest solution? Should the law seek above all to be fair or to be simple and easily understood? Would they accept a slight loss of their legal rights if it meant the Law became much easier to understand.

- Explain that the elimination of the automatic right to reject is aimed at simplifying the law, so the law becomes more in line with European Law. How, if at all, does this change their view?

SUM UP AND CLOSE - Collect questionnaires

APPENDIX B
PEOPLE AND ORGANISATIONS WHO MET US OR SENT SUBMISSIONS FROM JANUARY TO APRIL 2008

ACADEMIC LAWYERS

W Cowan H Ervine
Professor Geraint Howells
Professor JK Macleod
Dr Christian Twigg-Flesner
Professor Simon Whittaker

BUSINESS GROUPS

British Retail Consortium
British Shops and Stores Association Limited
Confederation of British Industry
Intellect – Consumer Electronics Council
Retail Motor Industry Federation
Scottish Motor Trade Association
Society of Motor Manufacturers and Traders Limited

CONSUMER GROUPS

Citizens Advice
Consumer Direct
Consumer Direct Scotland
LACORS (the Local Authorities Coordinators of Regulatory Services)
National Consumer Council (now Consumer Focus)
Scottish Consumer Council (now Consumer Focus Scotland)
Society of Chief Officers of Trading Standards in Scotland
UK European Consumer Centre
Which?

OTHER REPRESENTATIVE BODIES

City of London Law Society

Printed in the UK for The Stationery Office Limited
on behalf of the Controller of Her Majesty's Stationery Office
ID 5953306   11/08

Printed on Paper containing 75% recycled fibre content minimum.